the taste diaries

Michael Devlin

photography by Jude Browne

melting pot publications

Copyright **UlsterHerald** 2010
Copyright Photography Jude Browne and Michael Devlin
First published in 2010 by Melting Pot Publications

Design by Paperfuse and Michael Devlin

Typeset in American Typewriter and American Typewriter
light

Printed and bound by Commercial Graphics NI Ltd in
Northern Ireland

ISBN 978-0-9567280-0-5

Melting Pot Publications
77 Elmwood Green
Castlederg
Tyrone
BT817GZ

For Sarah

ACKNOWLEDGEMENTS

The list is long and distinguished. This book wouldn't have been possible without the best local newspaper in the world, the **Ulster**Herald. Therefore, to John, Niall (and his computer), Dominic (for giving me the go-ahead) and the scone/banana brigade, thanks for everything. To to my parents and particularly my mother for serving up some of the best nosh a boy could ask for, gratitude doesn't even begin to explain. To my friends and family, for all their beers of encouragement and free jars of jam from time to time, thanks a mill. To Adrian and Paperfuse for all the design advice; to Tricia and Paul for all the helpful hints; to Una and everyone at Lairdesgin; to all the good people at Commercial Graphics, thanks again. To Jude Browne for her dedication in the face of abject disorganisation, I still don't know how you managed to make some of my dishes look good, but there you go: The pix are class. The second time should be easier – boom boom! To Fivemiletown for the shards of loveliness; to Corsica and Jean-Charles for the inspiration; to Rory for the sound advice – keep up the good work everyone! And last but not least, to my wife and fellow gastronaut, Theresa (whom I haven't poisoned yet), thanks for making me do it and thanks for the salads and sammies. We must have dinner some time.

X

CONTENTS

so who's to blame?

A FRIEND of mine calls me 'Delia'. He thinks he's being funny, God love him. In fairness, I know he's only joking and I've certainly been called worse from time to time but why couldn't he have picked a male chef's moniker? Why not, Gordon or Jamie or Hugh? Because I'll tell you why: Even though this buddy of mine (who shall remain nameless) is only pulling my leg, there is an element of meaning in what he is suggesting.

I'm not saying that I'd rather be in a dress and waltz around at weekends introducing myself as Mandy however, in Northern Ireland in this year of our Lord 2010, men still don't do the cooking, it's as simple as that. The kitchen is seen as the domain of the fairer of the sexes and most men almost seem to take pride in their culinary ignorance.

"Beans on toast is about as fancy as I get, hi," is an oft heard statement when someone asks me what I'm cooking (this weather). And in fairness to these gents as well, there's nothing wrong with beans on toast, especially if you melt in a knob of butter, season well and add an unholy amount of grated cheese at the end.

It is, I think, an echo of generations past when men went out to work and the ladies stayed at home to look after the weans and have the dinner on the table for quitting time. Times have obviously changed and these days almost as many women work as men, but attitudes and notions are slow to turn. We're getting there, though. Slowly but ever so surely, the hairier of the sexes are venturing into the kitchen and lifting spoons and banging them against pots and pans and laughing at their mistakes (that's what I do anyway).

In truth, I don't know why more men don't cook or why more women don't take more pleasure in their time in the kitchen. Some of the most fun Sundays I have ever had were spent with a bottle of wine, some music and trying out a new recipe.

You know the saying, 'Nothing worthwhile was ever easy.' Well, it's wrong.

Half the recipes in this book are as easy as recipes come and they are the most worthwhile and gratifying experiences you can have cooking for yourself (especially if there's red wine and some tunes involved). All you have to do is try it. It's great craic, you get to have a snifter or two and even better, there's a great reward in the form of a pie or a stew at the end.

The whole idea for this cook book came about entirely by accident. It started one morning some years ago when my old editor at the Ulster**Herald**, Darach MacDonald called me into his office. It was like being called to see the head master and I half expected him to tell me I'd been slacking and it was time to pull up my journalistic socks. But not a bit of it.

"You like your food, Michael,' he said distractedly.

"Are you trying to say I is fat?" I wanted to say, but didn't.

"You don't fancy writing a piece for page 11 of the Scene. It doesn't have to be anything too detailed and we're not talking about cook book stuff. Give it a go and then we'll have a chat."

And that was that. All I knew was, it had to mention food and as well, if it got me out of court reporting, I was a happy man.

Almost half a decade later, the column on page 11 is still going, I am yet to run out of taste to talk about and they still aren't making me go to court. Result!

I decided to compile and organise this book mainly because I became fed up with people asking, "when's the cook book coming out?" And also, it will make for a good door stop if nothing else.

I'm not saying this is the perfect way to do things in a kitchen but rather, these recipes are what work for me. There's very little fanciness – if any at all – and the emphasis throughout is on taste rather than presentation. You might notice that some of the dishes look a little higglety-pigglety but rest assured, they taste a lot better than they look.

I hope you like it (the recipes etc) and if you don't then I'm blaming Darach.

one... something fishy

the right food at the right time
pan fried mackerel with potatoes

WE hear a lot about seasonal food these days and rightly so. Eating local produce makes infinitely more sense than buying stuff that's been flown half way around the world. Not only is the local fare obviously fresher (and thus tastier), the environment's a winner too since there are far less air miles involved.

Food writer, Nigel Slater once said that he couldn't imagine anyone wanting to eat asparagus on a winter's morning (or something along those lines) and I couldn't agree more. Supermarkets would have us believe that all produce should be available for all people at all times of the year, but this surely can't be right. The whole point about fresh food is the seasonality of stuff and the cyclical nature of vegetables becoming available as they ripen, game coming into season, harvesting herbs etc – it's just makes sense.

I think, however, we can take food that little step further. If you think about it, some foods just seem to suit the situation. Now, I'm not talking about restaurants or eating out, although somehow chicken fried rice just seems to 'suit' 2 o'clock in the morning – I'm referring to the food you'll eat at home, the things we prepare for ourselves. Fair play to them, restaurants often pander to seasonality but it isn't every night that we can afford to eat out.

What suits a summer Sunday morning when the sun is beaming down outside? Of course, it has to be a bowl of chopped fruit, apple, tangerine, grapes, mango and pineapple. When else would you have the time? Or, what would go best on a rainy

Tuesday night in November? Scotch broth with the consistency of thick porridge and buttery bread – no doubt. Or what about 4 in the morning when you should be in bed but hunger has forced you to stand, barefoot and in your boxers (or negligée, as the case may be), in the false dawn of your whirring fridge's light? It has to be cheese and pickle on stale bread with a glass of icy milk.

My point is, certain foods suit certain times and often we don't think about this, but when we do and when our stomachs and brains click together, it can mean the most wonderfully satisfying reaction.

Mackerel are generally available all year round but are probably at their best in late spring early summer and if you're lucky you'll get some fresh silver delight. As recipes go, this is as simple as they come; it's the combination which makes it. Mackerel is one of those fish which needs as little messing around with as possible. You will find plenty of recipes for curried mackerel or spiced mackerel or whatever, but the natural taste is what you want anyway. If it ain't broke, don't break it.

INGREDIENTS

2 mackerel
as many new potatoes as you like
1 small bunch of fresh dill
seasoned flour
pinch of cayenne
vegetable oil
40g unsalted butter
1 lemon/lime
salt

THE PLAN

Boil or steam the new potatoes until nice and tender. As this is happening, dust the mackerel fillets in the seasoned

flour (plus the pinch of cayenne) and shake off any excess. Heat the oil in a frying pan (medium heat) and half of the of the butter. When the butter is beginning to foam and sizzle, fry the mackerel for 3 minutes on each side then remove from the pan, cover and set aside.

Then, dump out the fish-frying oil from the pan. Add the remaining butter and heat through until it smells nutty. Squeeze the juice of half the lemon or lime into the pan, stir your impromptu sauce around and then pour over the fillets.

Season the mackerel with a little salt, sprinkle over the chopped dill and serve with the remaining half of the lemon wedges and the new potatoes.

But when to eat?

This should only happen on a warm Saturday night when you've returned from the beach with sand in your hair and salt on your lips. Slake your thirst with a cold beer (or three) as the potatoes slowly boil and then as you eat the toothsome meat, you'll be magically returned to the seaside. If you've managed to catch the fish yourself, you will feel like Poseidon. And if you're cooking these on the beach, you are Poseidon.

ales and tales about the one that didn't get away
potted salmon

I REMEMBER the time a fisherman friend caught a salmon, a big silver monster of a fish, glistening and bright, fresh out of the Atlantic. I can't recall the name of the artificial bait he said he hooked it on, but what made his feat all the more impressive was the fact that he created the lure himself. I was impressed anyway.

When he asked if I wanted it, I nearly took his hand off. But when I opened the package and laid the fish out on the kitchen table, I suddenly realised my dilemma: It was massive. Weighing in at over 5lbs, the salmon was a tiddler compared to the monster David landed the year before, which was over twice that size. Nevertheless, faced with the prospect of doing justice to such a mere 5lb fish, I was at a loss at where to begin.

Regarding it, beautifully stiff fresh and dazzling on my kitchen table I wondered and wondered. I rifled through cook books for inspiration but nothing jumped out at me.

These pots or ramekins or small mugs covered in cling-film should keep in the fridge for some time – the reason potting was invented was to preserve meats – but personally, I've never been able to 'preserve' mine for longer than 48 hours.

Blatantly wild (farmed salmon are chubbier and nowhere near as sleek), the fish could have been framed and mounted on a wall. Briefly I considered taking the easy route out of Dodge; chopping, bagging and freezing but then I reckoned it would be a shame to condemn such a fine fish to an unspecified purgatory in the freezer.

Would I share the love and farm some steaks out to friends and family? Possibly. Or would I eat the whole thing myself. Oh, yeah. And then it hit me. I would preserve it in one of the tastiest creations known to mankind: Butter.

I had made potted salmon only once before but it had been an unqualified success. There's nothing to it, really. All you need is some patience and the right ingredients and the clarifying of the butter is as hard as it gets.

As luck would have it, David came down to visit the night I was 'dealing' with the bounty so we made the most of the culinary windfall – it also provided him with the chance (over the course of several ales) to regale us with tales of 'the one that got away'.

I baked two steaks in the oven with a few lemon slices and knobs of butter and then we tucked into salmon carbonara, the creamy fresh version of the smoked recipe I mention later (keep reading). But the real star of the show was our potted friend.

INGREDIENTS

600g (or thereabouts) of salmon fillet(s)
500g of unsalted butter
bunch of spring onions (white parts only) finely chopped
clove of garlic, crushed
half tsp of salt
half tsp of either mace or cayenne pepper
tbsp of chopped chives or chopped parsley
good pinch of ground white pepper

THE PLAN

Clarify the butter: Heat said butter in a pan until it melts and foams. Remove from the heat and stand until the milky stuff sinks to the bottom, then strain your liquid gold through muslin. Give the bin the residue.

Now, trim up the salmon (de-skin etc) and cut into small cubes, dice-sized pieces. In a pan, heat the clarified butter until it simmers and then add the spring onions. Give these about a minute and then toss in the garlic, mace/cayenne pepper and salt and pepper. Dump in the salmon, taking care not to splash the whole hob, burning yourself in the process and turn the heat down a bit. Cook the cubes of fish until they have all changed colour, carefully moving them around a bit – this should take about four or five minutes. After that, remove from the heat, add the herbs and stir the cubes.

Spoon the salmon into the ramekins (the size of the moulds will determine how many you fill, but even one quarter of this fishy buttery delight would be enough to share between two people) and top up with the remaining butter to completely cover. Allow to cool and then chill in the fridge until set.

These pots or ramekins or small mugs covered in cling-film should keep in the fridge for some time – the reason potting was invented was to preserve meats – but personally, I've never been able to 'preserve' mine for longer than 48 hours. Spread on hot toast or hot wheaten bread with maybe a squeeze of lemon juice and soon you'll be considering fabricating lures and joining Dave on the river-bank.

surf and turf, well kind of
smoked fish with poached egg

IF the culinary equivalent of Desert Island Discs was ever invented, I reckon poached eggs on toast would feature pretty highly on my list. It's one of the few dishes that I really have to limit myself eating, otherwise I'd be breakfasting, lunching, dining and snacking on them without ever getting fed up – or full up.

Even back in the day, my mother used to warn me that scoffing too many eggs would lead to a peculiar digestive condition she only ever referred to as 'egg bun'. She never exactly said what this meant, only that it was a fate worse than extinction. Though with hindsight, I think this was kind of scare tactics on her part to keep me away from the eggs – which I continued to devour nonetheless, somehow managing to avoid the dreaded malady.

Unpretentious, easy to make, ultra-satisfying and immensely nutritious (if you use wholemeal bread), the poaching variation of the humble egg is even today a huge source of wonderment for me; that something so simple can be so delicious. You don't have to do anything fancy for it to be class; the unadulterated flavour of the eggs is the best thing, although a great variation on the same theme is replacing the normal hen's egg with a duck egg.

Stronger and in fact much tastier than the common hen egg, a duck egg is an altogether different animal (bird) – so-much-so, that once you've tasted a poached duck egg, it's hard to return to the blander hen offspring.

The following recipe (which for me is basically just an excuse to eat poached eggs), smoked fish with a duck egg, is only worth having if you can find proper smoked white fish (ie not the ridiculous yellow dyed stuff). If you can't find naturally smoked fish, just have the duck egg on toast, only leave out the rocket. You won't be disappointed.

Contrary to popular belief, there's nothing to poaching an egg without all the plastic kit nonsense. All you need is some white wine vinegar and a little vigilance. The vinegar stops the egg from disintegrating.

INGREDIENTS

1 large fresh duck egg
1 large slice of bread, the choice is yours
butter
white wine vinegar
1 fillet of any smoked white fish, cod, halibut, pollock, whiting etc
full fat milk
bay leaf
big handful of rocket leaves

THE PLAN

First of all, place your skinless fillet of smoked fish along with the bay leaf in a pan and just cover with the milk. Put a lid on and bring almost to the boil and then take it off the heat. The residual heat in the pan will be enough to cook the fish through and it's cooked when it flakes easily and comes apart in your hands.

When this is ready, keep it warm whilst you bring another medium sized pan of water to the boil. Add two capfuls of the vinegar (slightly less than a table-spoonful) and when it starts to boil, turn the heat down to the minimum setting.

You want this water to be very slightly simmering – almost not bubbling at all.

When the water is ready, crack your egg onto a saucer and then slide it (the egg) gently into the water. It should sink happily to the bottom.

As soon as it's in, start your bread to toasting. You should find that as soon as the bread has toasted, and you've buttered it, the egg will be ready; the white will have set but the yolk will still be soft.

Remove with a slotted spoon and drain carefully.

Now layer it up. Put the buttered toast on a plate, cover with the rocket, add the fish, a sprinkling of salt and black pepper and then the freshly poached egg, followed by another pinch of seasoning.

Forget about all your fancy wines for this one. There's only one thing you have to have, and that's a big mug of milky tea. Unbeatable for breakfast or lunch or even dinner.

Egg bun, here I come.

---

remember to flex your muscles
moules mariniere

AS comforting as the most soothing bowl of chicken soup ever created and yet at the same time as tantalising and as sophisticated as the finest freshly prepared sushi, there exists, a dish of such heavenly delight, it's almost dangerous. The main problem is, however, everyone seems to have forgotten about it.

Garnering a bad rep from people who don't know any better, mussels are often regarded as poor man's shellfish. Granted they're plentiful and cheap but with the right preparation and a bit of imagination, the little slate-coloured bullets are arguably better than oysters or even scallops.

In the wild, mussels grow on coastline rocks and stony outcrops although they are also farmed off suitable coastal waters. Scottish waters are exemplary for mussels to develop and mature and, indeed, have quite a long and illustrious history with the Scottish peasantry. It was even commonplace for fishwives to offer them as street food, setting up little stalls selling the bountiful harvest in saucers with a little cooking soup. Nowadays, chefs go a little further in helping the average mussel attain a certain culinary level but the idea is still the same.

Most of us live little more than an hour away from the brine-tinted air and yet you'd think it was light years into the future – or the past. We appear to have abandoned the humble mussel in favour of other Johnny-come-latelys, namely tiger prawns and the imported masses.

And the best of it is, if you have a penchant for the little balls of seaside taste, you can even pick them up at the coast for nothing. Though be warned (arrr!): If you do collect your own mussels, make sure the waters are unpolluted and avoid hunting for them in the warmer weather as mussels are only in season where there is an 'r' in the month.

There are many different ways to cook the mussel from baking to steaming to roasting, you only have to look at any online cooking resource to see that there are literally hundreds of recipes to chose from.

Say what you like about them but the French generally know how to fling some food together and their quintessential method for mussels is Moules Mariniere. Classic, simple and infinitely tasty and the best news is, it couldn't be handier.

Often bags of mussels in a supermarket or fishmongers come in 1kg sizes so that's the one I'll give you the recipe for. It's easily enough for a main course for two people but I find they're like Pringles... once you pop.

INGREDIENTS

1kg (slightly over 2 pounds) fresh mussels
big knob of butter
little knob of butter
half a glass of white wine
2 spring onions, chopped (you could also use a couple of shallots or at a pinch, even an onion)
100 ml (or there abouts) double cream
1 tbsp chopped parsley and/or chives
1 clove of garlic (optional).
1 bay leaf

LE PLAN D'ACTION

Rinse the mussels in running water and get rid of any beardy stuff or any that are open. Heat the big knob of butter in a large pan. When it's foaming add the spring onions or shallots or whatever (and the garlic if you're using it) and the bay leaf and cook gently until they're soft.

Turn the heat up to high, bang in the mussels and wine and cover. Cook flat out for two to three minutes or until the mussels have opened – keep an eye on them and give the pan the odd shake from time to time to help it along.

After that, strain the mussels, keeping the cooking liquor but binning any of the little fellas that haven't opened.

Return the cooking juices to the pan, add the little knob of butter, the cream and the herbs and bring to the simmer to thicken slightly.

To finish, pour the tasty broth over the mussels and serve with crusty bread and a pint of stout (or even a glass of white wine).

These are utterly fantastic. You'll even be tempted to eat the shells.

salmon and oxymorons
fish carbonara

I REMEMBER once Billy Connolly thought it hilarious that a recipe in a cookbook said, "Perfect for all that left-over venison." You see, I was about to say that this next recipe is perfect for all your left-over smoked salmon, but then reckoned it something of an oxymoron.

Anyway, this recipe is perfect for any left over smoked salmon you might have, or if you're like me and you only buy smoked salmon to order, then it's well worth the purchase. Also, since the dish only uses the smallest amount of salmon, one of the tiny packs will be more than sufficient.

You could say this is the seafood equivalent of normal carbonara. It's the quickness of pasta which makes it so appealing for me, that and the fact that a sumptuous meal takes about 15 minutes to prepare.

This recipe came about by accident after a holiday to France. The missus had 'creamy salmon pasta' at one of the many excellent local restaurants in Nice and I tried to replicate it at home.

Unfortunately, I'm told this dish is nothing like the original version (possibly since I used smoked salmon instead of fresh), but fortunately, it still tastes great. Moreover, the original recipe included asparagus tips, but I've left these out, since the ones from Peru only taste of air-miles (when ours aren't in season). It also included a teaspoonful of caviar, but I didn't have any left over. In my dreams.

INGREDIENTS (serves two)

75g of smoked salmon, sliced into thin strips
160g of linguine (any kind of pasta would work)
150g of creme fraiche
2 tablespoons of chopped chives
1 clove of garlic, chopped
2 spring onion, chopped (just the white parts)
2 tablespoons of lemon juice
handful of grated parmesan
olive oil
white pepper

THE PLAN

First set your pasta to boiling in plenty of salted boiling water. Whilst this is going, sweat your garlic and spring onions in a splash of olive oil. Do this on a medium to low heat because you don't want the garlic to colour at all. About five minutes should do it.

Next dump the crème fraiche into the pan with the parmesan, simmer and stir until the cheese has melted and then stir in the salmon, lemon juice and half the chives. Mix it up and take off the heat. At this stage it should smell divine.

As soon as the pasta is ready, drain and dump into the pan of sauce and toss until it's all coated, shimmering and lovely. Give it a grating of white pepper and taste for salt, then divide between two bowls. Sprinkle over the remaining chives, an extra drizzle of olive oil and another pinch of parmesan and that's it.

This is a great, quick supper when you're in need of a blast of sunshine on a grey evening. And the garlic bread would make a good mop if you can be bothered.

Now all we have to do is invent a pasta dish for the left-over venison – as soon as I win the lottery.

this recipe is perfect for any left over smoked salmon you might have, or if you're like me and you only buy smoked salmon to order, then it's well worth the purchase.

VARIATIONS

A handful of peas would another dimension, as would the asparagus when it's in season.

Dill would make a good alternative to chives and flatleaf parsley would work at a pinch. You could even try fresh salmon as opposed to the smoked variety and supplement double cream for the fraiche.

THERE'S used to be an advert running on the telly for Simply Bake to Perfection, Birdseye's new "revolutionary" Bake Perfect Bag™ range for fish.

"Simply Bake to Perfection gives you a mouth-watering meal every time without the effort," the blurb on the website reads.

"Our revolutionary Bake Perfect Bag™ means that all you need to do is pop in the oven for 20-25 minutes and everything else is done for you. No touching raw fish, no unwanted aromas. Just perfectly cooked delicious mouth-watering meals without the fuss."

What fuss? Taking the salmon or cod fillets out of the fridge and wrapping in tinfoil? Squeezing on a drop of lemon juice? It seems to me our big commercial brothers are trying to sanitise cooking in the name of convenience. "No touching raw fish, no unwanted aromas."

God forbid you might have to touch your own dinner as you cook it. And what unwanted aromas?

Birdseye's Grub in a Bag™ might well taste good but I bet my bottom dollar I could make far better fish with just the tiniest extra effort. There's nothing to it, in fact, if you can make a Christmas cracker shape out of the tinfoil, you're home and dry.

SALMON FILLET NUMBER ONE: Lemon and garlic and dill

(There is no ingredients list, 'cause it's not very technical).

Depending on the size of the fillet it will take between 14 and 20 minutes to cook but always err on the side of caution and check it after 14. If it flakes and looks cooked, it is.

Drip some olive oil onto a square of tin foil, rub it around and lay on the salmon fillet. Sprinkle on some chopped dill, a few thinly sliced shards of garlic and a good squeeze of lemon – plus a little rind. Add a knob of butter, form into the afore-mentioned cracker and blast in a medium oven (190°C) for 14 minutes.

SALMON FILLET NUMBER TWO: Honey and lemon and soy and garlic and olive oil.

In a separate bowl, combine 1 tablespoon of honey, two of soy sauce, half a clove or garlic (crushed), the juice of half a lemon and about 4 tablespoonfuls of good extra virgin olive oil. Mix around and then drop in the salmon fillet. Marinate for 15 or 20 minutes and then again, drip some olive oil onto your square of tin foil, rub it around and lay on the salmon fillet. Add some more marinating mix, cracker it up and blast in the oven.

SALMON FILLET NUMBER THREE: Parmesan and pesto and breadcrumbs

Basically you want to coat the top of the fillet with your mixture. So in a bowl combine a dollop of green pesto (preferably home-made, *see page 79*), a small handful of breadcrumbs and the same of grated parmesan. Add a touch of olive oil and a little seasoning and then, as I said, spread this over the top of the salmon fillet. There's no need to wrap this one up, just blast it in the oven for the appropriate time and dig in.

Alongside some simply boiled potatoes or a handful of chips or some dressed salad leaves, and these salmon examples are essential summer taste. And of course, these are only suggestions.

And, I've had another brainwave. I'm going to call it, Michael's Perfect Fish Idea™. What about this: If you don't like the aroma of fish, don't eat it.

Genius ™.

so you think you don't like anchovies?
jansson's temptation

THE world is divided into two groups of people: Those who love anchovies and those who only think they don't like them.

Mostly, when a certain recipe calls for these little members of the herring family I won't even tell the missus I'm using them, lest she turn up her nose and ask if her portion can be anchovy-free. Normally, I'll just bung them in and say nothing and normally she won't even notice (in lamb stew for example, the anchovies will melt away entirely). Some times though, I'll say, "What do you think of this dish or that dish?" And if we get two thumbs up, I'll say, "Haha! The whole thing's full of anchovies."

There are some dishes however where there's no denying the little fishy presence. Jansson's temptation, for example is only possible with anchovies and loads of them. Fortunately, the finished product is beyond delicious and if you have anyone in the house who only thinks they don't like anchovies, this is the recipe to turn them.

Factoid: This Swedish classic is actually traditionally made with pickled sprats and the fallacy with anchovies came about because sprats, pickled in sugar and salt. However, in the Devlin household anchovies work just fine and if you ever get around to trying this dish, you'll understand.

Legend has it, Jansson's temptation got its name from the story that this was the meal that tempted Jansson, a religious fanatic to renounce his vow to give up earthly pleasures – and again, it you ever get around to trying it, you'll understand.

In reality, it's probably called Jansson's temptation because Jansson is such a popular name in Sweden therefore, it's everyone's temptation.

INGREDIENTS

1 small can of anchovies in olive/sunflower oil (50g or thereabouts)
4 big spuds –I used Roosters (450gs or thereabouts), peeled and thinly sliced
1 big onion or two small ones, sliced
good glug of double cream (5 tbs or thereabouts)
loads of freshly ground black pepper
chopped parsley, to serve

THE PLAN

This is almost embarrassingly simple to make and the aforementioned ingredients will be enough for two as a main supper dish or four as a side.

Start off by setting your oven to heating at 200°C (possibly slightly cooler if you have a fan oven).

Open the anchovy can and drip out all the oil into a large frying pan or wok. Add the onions and cook over a medium heat for 5 or 10 minutes without colouring too much until softened – it should smell delicious even at this early stage.

As the onions are sweating, peel your spuds and finely chop them into matchstick chips. You want really thin chips, like thick match sticks.

When the onions are soft, add the super-thin chips to the pan and stir about to coat with all the lovely onion-y and fish-y juices. Fry for another 5 or 10 minutes until the spuds start to go limp and then remove from the heat. Add the anchovies, chopped into smaller pieces and the cream and a good grinding of black pepper and stir everything up really well.

Load your tempting bounty into a shallow ovenproof dish and retire to the oven for at least 30 minutes. Check after 20 minutes and if the top is browning but the chips are nowhere near soft, wrap a sheet of tin foil around it and give it another 10 minutes and test again. Test every ten minutes until tender and then check the seasoning. It shouldn't need much salt, if any, the anchovies will take care of that.

Spoon into big bowls, sprinkle on the parsley and dive in.

Who doesn't like anchovies now?

legend has it, Jansson's temptation got its name from the story that this was the meal that tempted Jansson, a religious fanatic to renounce his vow to give up earthly pleasures – and again, it you ever get around to trying it, you'll understand

the right side of poncy
kedgeree

I USED to watch The Great British Menu of an evening, if there was nothing else interesting on the box. It as just the right side of entertaining but still, I found it all a bit poncy; like, for example, having five different desserts on the same plate, each one a different take on strawberries: compote, jus, creme anglaise, biscuit, waffle – what's that all about?

I suppose it's a cookery programme after all, isn't it and ultimately a contest to create something new and innovative – as poncy as that new thing might be.

The blurb from the BBC press office reads, "Over the past three years, Great British Menu has cooked for Her Majesty The Queen at her 80th birthday banquet (poncy), served a magnificent meal to the gastronomic elite of France (tres poncy) and thrilled some of the world's finest chefs with some of the very best, cutting-edge contemporary British food (awfully, awfully, poncy, what-what, old bean!)."

As I say, it's all a bit poncy. The whole thing smacks of what I like to call, scientific cooking. Fat Duck, Heston Blumenclown-style stuff. The thing is: I have no doubt that what the competing chefs are cooking is some of the finest culinary morsels that a mere mortal will ever ingest. But for Joe and Josephine Public, the mere mortals on the street, these morsels might as well be served at a restaurant on the moon.

The other thing is: A dish I always considered a bit poncy and a mission to boot, kedgeree, is, as is happens, not half the trouble I ever imagined. And now that I've actually got around to cooking it, it no longer qualifies as poncy – not that it ever was.

A strange melange of eastern and western cuisines, kedgeree originated from Scotland and was taken to India by Scottish troops during the British Raj, where it was adapted and adopted as part of Indian cuisine. Traditionally, smoked haddock is used but nothing is set in stone.

Kedgeree couldn't be easier to make and is perfect for a late Sunday morning breakfast or even brunch. This is a recipe adapted from Darina Allen's Easy Entertaining but as usual, I didn't have half the ingredients required. By substituting and improvising however, it turned out remarkably well. I suppose it's the method that counts, really.

INGREDIENTS (Serves three)

hot smoked salmon, two fillets thereof, flaked
packet of microwave rice, the brown kind
two eggs, preferably organic and free range, hard boiled and quartered
125 ml of cream

> ...a strange melange of eastern and western cuisines, kedgeree originated from Scotland and was taken to India by Scottish troops during the British Raj, where it was adapted and adopted as part of Indian cuisine.

knob of butter
pinch of chilli flakes
tablespoon of chives
pinch of cayenne pepper
white bread for toasting

THE PLAN

The hot-smoked salmon (which is available almost everywhere but if you can't find it, any smoked fish will do), should only need a blast in the microwave. So blast the rice and the salmon, flake the fish and set aside. Heat the butter and the milk in a sauce pan with the chives, and chilli flakes and as soon as it start to bubble, remove from the heat, dump in the rice and flaked salmon and mix thoroughly but gently. Season well with salt and pepper and that pinch of cayenne and transfer to bowls. Add the quartered eggs and serve immediately, with plenty of buttered toast.

Sesame Street has been brought to you today by the word poncy.

as a youngster I remember off-setting the damage garlic could do to my chances with the fairer sex, with the notion that if I was ever attacked by a vampire, he or she would almost certainly find me unpalatable

two... our daily bread

keeping the bloodsuckers at bay
garlic bread

AS a youngster I remember off-setting the damage garlic could do to my chances with the fairer sex, with the notion that if I was ever attacked by a vampire, he or she would almost certainly find me unpalatable. My main weakness, which remains to this day, is garlic bread, with oodles of butter and flat-leaf parsley. Come to think of it, this was one of the first recipes I ever felt the need to create.

Garlic (Allium sativum) has traditionally been regarded by common-folk as a force for both good and evil. A Christian myth recounts that after Satan (or the 'Divil', as he is known in Ireland) left the Garden of Eden, garlic arose in his left footprint, and onion in the right.

Across Europe, various cultures have used garlic for protection or white magic, perhaps because of its reputation as a potent preventative medicine. Central European folk beliefs in particular, considered garlic a powerful ward against demons, werewolves, and the undead. To ward off vampires, garlic could be worn, hung in windows or rubbed on chimneys and keyholes. Alternatively, you could make a big loaf of garlic bread and consume it all Sunday long – this was and is, a mandatory requirement if there's a scary movie on the telly that night.

Historically, garlic originated from either India or somewhere in central Asia and is one of the oldest cultivated plants. Cherished the world over, it is believed that the plant first made it's way this far north because of the Romans. A fine little tit-bit of information is this: The term for 'leper' in the Middle Ages was 'pilgarlic' because the unfortunate leper would have to peel his own.

With a veritable myriad of uses, both culinary and medicinal, garlic is an ever present army in my kitchen. Whether I'm dropping whole cloves around roasts, rubbing salad bowls with a peeled bullet or making my own fresh pesto sauce. Essentially, the longer pungent garlic is cooked, in whatever form, the milder the flavour is likely to be. A fine tip I have discovered and now practise religiously is removing the green filaments within garlic cloves as the summer months roll in. I reckon this helps the taste but apparently, it also makes the garlic more digestible.

After the onion, garlic is the second most cultivated allium in the world. Everyone knows what it tastes like, even if you're not overly partial to the stuff. If you are a fan, you'll most likely know that fresh, or reasonably fresh garlic, is a world away in terms of taste from the supermarket stuff. And the good news on this front, is that it is super-easy to grow your own.

Traditionally planted on the shortest day of the year and harvested on the longest, growing garlic is (almost) child's play. For garden cultivation (plant in full sun and rich soil), split a bulb and insert the cloves pointed end up one inch deep and six inches apart. Then just make sure they're well watered and come

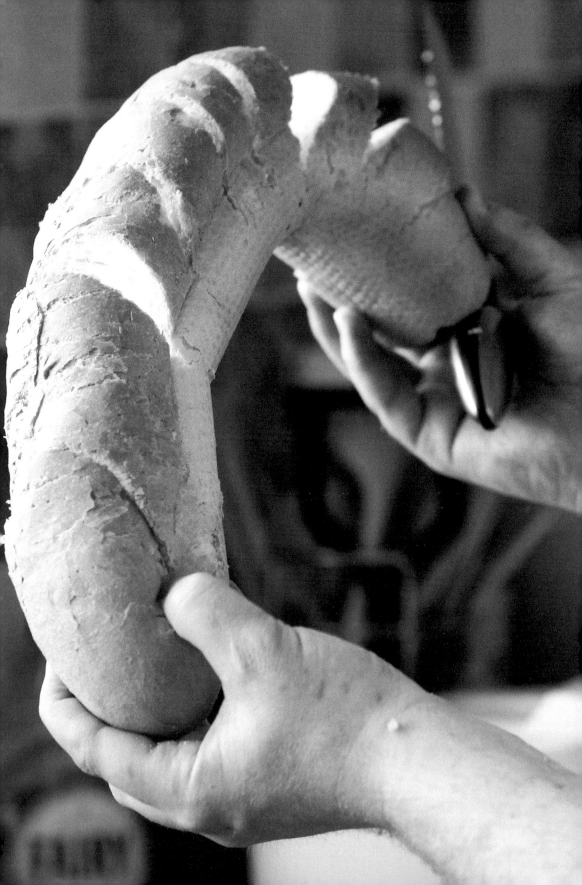

the end of the summer or beginning of autumn, they'll be well matured when the top growth starts to change colour and collapse. When harvest time arrives, ease the bulbs out of the soil and let them dry for a day or two (preferably in the sun).

For that lethal garlic bread I mentioned earlier, it couldn't be simpler.

INGREDIENTS

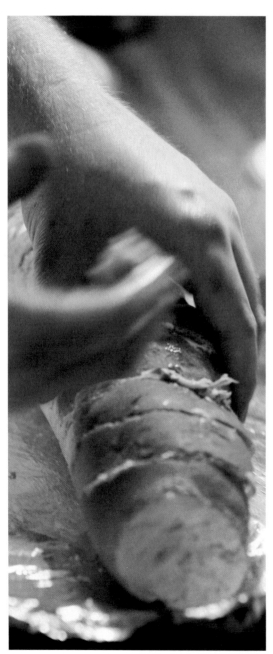

1 loaf (use ciabatta, baguette or bloomer for best results)
2/3 cloves of garlic depending on their size
big handful of chopped flat leaf parsley
pinch of salt
twist of black pepper
two ounces of butter (at least – but basically, you can use as much as you like).

THE PLAN

Crush and mash the garlic on a chopping board with your pinch of salt. Add this mix to the butter and thoroughly mix. Fling in your chopped parsley and the twist of black pepper.

Cut your chosen loaf into (almost) diagonal slices, at a 45 degree angle – but don't cut all the way through. Put a big glob of butter between each semi-slice and then smear any remaining butter across the top of the loaf. Wrap in tinfoil and bake in a hot oven (220-°C) for 15 to 20 minutes. The crust should be crispy and the bread within golden and unctuous.

Delicious, soul-food and perfect for late night comfort.

Keeps the blood suckers at bay, too.

- bonjour monsieur!
- bonjour madam!
- croque monsieur

IT'S one of the culinary matches forged in heaven, and like the wheel, it's difficult to imagine life without ham and cheese. So ubiquitous is the celestial combination, we have even began to take it for granted.

Good quality ham with cheddar (or Emmental, Edam, Mozzarella – the variations are endless) on crusty bread with real butter and a twist of salt and black pepper is rustic, wholesome and immensely satisfying. Add a touch of mayonnaise and honey and mustard and it's onto another level. Apply some heat to the equation and we're going stratospheric. Sometimes we tend to forget that simple things can often be the best.

I was first introduced to a croque-monsieur in Strasbourg circa 1992 and since then, despite our ups and downs, seeing other people and the like, we have enjoyed a passionate and hungry relationship. If you've ever had intimate relations with a croque, you'll know how inherently classy, chic and decadent they can be.

Yet the best thing about them is their simplicity. In terms of preparability, you can have a croque cooked and on your table in under 10 minutes and in so far as flavour goes, croques always taste like you momentarily morphed into a certain Mr Ramsey.

Essentially, a croque-monsieur is a hot ham and cheese (typically Gruyère) grilled sandwich and as is always the case with popular food, there are infinite variations on the same theme. Gypsy-croques can be dipped in beaten egg, then pan-fried in butter and a croque-monsieur served with a fried egg on top is known as a croque-madame. I've even had one with pears and brie, although I'm not too sure what it was called – but whatever the case, the cheese and ham element is ever-present.

Originating in France as a fast-food snack served in cafés and bars, the name (croque-monsieur) is based on the verb 'croquer' which means 'to crunch' or 'to bite hungrily' and the word 'monsieur' – mister – the reason behind the combination of the two words is unclear. But who cares.

If you never try another recipe as long as you live, you have to give this one a go. In fact, you don't even have to know anything about cooking, so simple and straightforward is the recipe, it's hardly even a recipe at all. As simple as assembling a sandwich, this is the epitome of quick and easy. Basically, if you can toast bread and grate cheese, then you're laughing all the way to Tasteville – and you're the mayor.

The owner of a tiny place called 'Le Sandwicherie' in the mountain town of Corté in Corsica told me how to make this particular croque. I remember Jean-Claude looking at me a little strangely when I asked how to make it. I soon realised why, it should have been self explanatory.

INGREDIENTS (for one)

Two slices of white bread, lightly toasted
Two or three shards of ham, the best stuff you can find
Dollop of creme fraiche
Two handfuls of grated cheese (Gruyere, cheddar or any melting cheese. you could even try different combinations)
Salt and pepper

THE PLAN

Butter your toasted bread and set the grill to high. As this warms, make a normal sandwich with the ham (I always put a few crumbs of cheese in for the craic). Then, in a bowl, mix one handful of the cheese with your dollop of creme fraiche and season well. Spread this on top of your ham sandwich, sprinkle on your other handful of cheese (cover the whole thing) and bang it under the grill.

Keep an eye on the croque and when the cheese starts to turn golden brown, it's ready. It should smell amazing but be warned: I've lost count of the number of times I've burned the roof of my mouth on one of these toasties – probably every time I've had one – so be careful, the creme fraiche/cheese mix will be molten succulence.

Eat with a knife and fork and several amorous sighs.

IF there's one area of culinary exploration I have yet to fully appreciate, it has to be baking. It's not that I don't enjoy the end product; it's just that baking isn't exactly immediate gratification and furthermore, it isn't type of cooking where you just fling stuff together, haphazard and slap dash, chef Picasso style. It's all very measured and precise and you even have to use scales! For the uninitiated, it's just all a bit daunting.

And yet, from the limited time I have spent baking (which seems to increase as I get older and less energetic), there is something very homely and relaxing about kneading bread and waiting for the yeast to activate and rise. It might not be magical exactly but it's definitely food for the soul. Come to think of it, it's not dissimilar to the feeling you get when you harvest your own gnarly looking vegetables. Effort, nature, reward.

Luckily, for the baking inept (ie me), there are certain domes of excellence which take very little planning, the minimum in effort and the maximum in reward. Providing you have a set of weighing scales, an oven that works and the correct ingredients, scones are foolproof and the best of it is, you won't even destroy the kitchen in the process.

INGREDIENTS (MAKES A LOT)

220g self-raising flour
1 level tsp baking powder (optional)
50g butter
25g caster sugar
1 egg
130ml full fat milk (or there abouts)

THE PLAN

Preheat the oven to 220C/425F/Gas7 and lightly butter two baking trays. Break out the scales and measure the flour and baking powder and sift into a bowl, then add the butter and rub in with your fingertips until the mixture resembles fine breadcrumbs. If, at this stage, it looks nothing like breadcrumbs and more resembles a mess, don't worry just keep gently rubbing and it'll come round eventually. Then stir in the caster sugar.

Crack the egg into a measuring jug, then make up to 150ml/5fl oz with the milk. Mix this up and then stir into the flour - you may not need it all - but what you're looking for is a soft but not overly sticky dough.

Turn out on to a lightly floured work surface, knead very lightly and then roll out to a thickness of 2cm/1inch. The key here is not to over work the dough otherwise the scones won't rise and they'll turn out more like biscuits (though they'll still be edible).

Cut into rounds with a fluted cutter and place them on the prepared baking

trays.

Personally, I kind of like the way the scones will burst at the sides and turn into misshapen toadstools but if you don't want this to happen, don't twist the cutter as you cut them out. Just press down, lift away and knock off.

Before they go into the oven, brush the tops with a little extra milk, or dust with flour or even any egg and milk left in the jug, and bake in the oven for about 10 minutes or until they are risen and a pale golden brown. Lift onto a wire rack to cool slightly.

Scones are best eaten as fresh as possible, so if you're making this many, you'll need a few extra mouths to feed. With a dollop of strawberry jam and another of clotted cream, and a big mug of tea, scones are so tasty it's almost emotional. The only problem you'll have is limiting yourself to one or two.

VARIATIONS

For wheaten scones just replace 4oz of the self raising flour with whole-wheat flour. Or, for something a little more savoury, add a handful of grated cheddar and maybe a few crispy bacon bits to the batter before your turn it out onto the floured surface.

Or, for maximum fruitiness, instead of the cheese, add a handful of mixed dried fruits – raisins, sultanas or whatever.

Or, what about some chopped apple and a pinch of cinnamon for a winter warmer. Or maybe some a teaspoonful of dried oregano and some chopped sun-dried tomatoes for the Med effect.

Whatever the variation, once you've tasted your own freshly baked scones, pre-packed others will never come close again.

All I need now is a pipe, a pair of slippers and a copy of The People's Friend.

just top up and serve
bruschetta

I HONESTLY don't know how I lived before I started eating bruschetta. It's the handiness aspect of course, and the fact that it's ready to rock and on your plate within seconds of you dragging yourself across the threshold. But it's not just that. Sometimes, nothing else will do and because you can combine a multitude of flavours and mix and match and experiment, it's all the more fun.

If you've been living under a stone (or in a padded cell) for the past few years and haven't tried bruschetta yet, then pay close attention because your life is about to change.

In a nutshell, bruschetta is toasted bread flavoured with garlic, olive oil and whatever other tastes tickle any fancy at any given time. A perfect way of using left over meats or ripe vegetables about to turn the 'use-by' corner; bruschetta is also quick and perfectly fool proof.

You can have them small as appetisers along with a cold beverage or even pizza size if you can find a big enough loaf (with several cold beverages). There is only one golden rule: The better the olive oil, the better the bruschetta.

I can't recommend this stuff highly enough.

TO START

To make the base for the toppings it couldn't be simpler. Toast a slice of loaf (ciabatta, bloomer or whatever you lay your hands on) and as soon as it comes out of the toaster or from under the grill (or from maximum effect from the barbecue), rub the surface of the toast with a peeled clove of garlic. You can make it as strong or as light as you like, but as you rub you'll notice the clove shrinking. Then place the juvenile bruschetta on a plate and drizzle liberally with olive oil.

That's basically it.

You can even eat it as it is, with a sprinkling of sea salt but for maximum effect try one of these combos: Mozzarella and green pesto or feta cheese and red pesto or chopped tomatoes and some torn basil or diced bacon and grated cheddar.

Essentially, whatever you'd normally eat on a sandwich why not try it as a bruschetta topping? And once you've toasted the bread, that's all the cooking. Just top up and serve.

PIZZA MODE

This recipe is as quick as taking a frozen pizza out of the oven and heating it up but as far as taste goes, this is on a different planet. And not only does it taste good, it is also seriously impressive, aromatic and fantastic when you serve it up.

I won't give you a list of ingredients, since what you put on it is entirely up to you. So, for argument's sake, I'll mention what I stick on.

Find the biggest loaf you can get you hands on and cut off a thick slice from the fattest part. Grill this slice on both sides, rub with garlic and drizzle with oil. Now you have the pizza base.

Next, you can either use a jar of tomato pasta sauce or pizza topping or just make your own (glug of good olive oil in a pan, sizzle garlic slices for 10 seconds and dump in a can of tomatoes with a pinch of sugar and oregano. Reduce on a low heat for about 20 minutes until is resembles a sauce and then season – obviously you'll have you have this pre-prepared).

Spread your sauce over the pizza/bruschetta base (less is more) and then sprinkle with your favourite cheese (in this case, I'd be using cow's milk mozzarella and parmesan), some torn basil and maybe a slice of pepperoni or six.

Blast in a hot oven (220°C) for about 10 minutes or until the cheese is bubbly and irresistible and the bruschetta is slightly charred around the edges.

Another little drizzle of olive oil and some black pepper and a few torn leaves of basil and you'll wonder where this stuff has been living all your life.

With a green salad and a big glass of gutsy shiraz, this is unbelievably good.

---

nice inspired salmon sarnie

MY father always said that the best thing about going on holiday is the coming home again. And you know, I think he might be right.

A couple of years ago, on a holiday to Corsica and the South of France (eating and drinking my way along the Cote d'azure), digestively and for the good of my liver and heart, it was great to make it back. It may be one of the tastiest ingestions known to mankind but there's only so much foie gras one person can eat – and I never thought I'd hear myself say that.

Wines, cheeses, sausages, pâtés, croissants, caviar, coffee, baguettes, lobster, charcuterie, ice-creams, beer and even veal, each day on the Cote d'Azure was based around meal times. When we were eating breakfast (normally around midday) I was considering what would be on the menu for lunch and when we were eating lunch and thinking about dinner, I still hadn't properly digested breakfast.

Culinary pounding after culinary pounding, my stomach was rumbling for the wrong reasons from the third day but because of the delectability of the gastronomy on offer, I couldn't help myself.

And yet now, safe within the sanctuary of Gaviscon and mild Irish weather, I can look back on the whole experience with a whiff of rose tinted water. It was great, tough on the gut but great nonetheless.

Paradoxically, as soon as I returned home to Irish rain, I felt myself looking forward to the chills of autumn and winter and the necessary hearty fare these seasons demand. Not that we ever have much of a summer to mention, but there's only so many Salades Nicoises a northern stomach can take.

As I write this in September, there has also been a slight bite to the morning air these past few days which has made me yearn for a big bowl of Scotch Broth and some buttery wheaten bread – but that's a story for another time.

Even more paradoxically, I remember when I returned home from Provence, my consumption of baked beans and Tayto Spring Onion crisp sandwiches sky-rocketed.

Of course, the old phenomenon still holds: The further and longer an Irish person departs from Ireland the more Irish that person actually becomes. We yearn for spuds and stout and bacon sarnies form a greasy spoon.

But apart from bacon rolls and the like, even more appealing for me when I return home from holidays is salmon sandwiches.

"– Oh, la dee da! Hear yer man, eating his salmon and caviar and Paris buns, who does he think he is, Elvis?"

culinary pounding after culinary pounding, my stomach was rumbling for the wrong reasons from the third day but because of the delectability of the gastronomy on offer, I couldn't help myself.

The thing is, I don't normally eat that much salmon; it's a bit on the dear side and if you go for the cheapest smoked stuff it tastes like yellow rubber.

However, I have discovered a little sandwich which, prepared with a little care and attention is plain, tasty, practically unbeatable and very Irish – well kind of.

INGREDIENTS (makes one huge sarnie)

1 salmon steak cooked and flaked
2 slices of white bread,
dollop of crème fraiche
another of mayo
salt and pepper
grated lemon (or lime) rind and a squeeze of the juice.

Assemble as you normally would a sarnie, butter the bread first, layer on some creme fraiche on one slice, the mayo on another, add the grated rind, then the salmon, squeeze the juice, season and eat without delay.

This sandwich will make you feel like you are on holiday in Ireland and if you find yourself on holiday in France, you won't go wrong either.

three... saturday nights

irish tapas
crispy potato skins

EVEN spuds can exist beyond the culinary line I have etched in the sand when I'm stumbling across the threshold on a weekday evening. Sometimes all you want is a maid and a cook – is that too much to ask?

Saturday nights on the other hand... for some reason, Saturday night lends itself to gastronomic creation like no other, especially if it involves friends and family and a fridgeful of bottles of suds. Grazing on snacks in between doling out the drinks is a form of eating on its own.

This next recipe is well worth the effort – although perhaps not on a Tuesday. Crispy potato skins are time consuming and labour intensive so you'll either have to have plenty of time on your hands or have the butler do it. For some reason I find these crisps the perfect accompaniment to Saturday evening beer. It takes two bottles to get past prep stage and just when you're tottering along the cliffs of starvation, the oven finally pays out.

INGREDIENTS

spuds (I normally use roosters or maris pipers for this one, though the quantity is hard to define. Three normal sized spuds per person should to the trick). Old spuds, ie ones with thick skins work best
melted butter
salt and pepper

THE PLAN

Puncture your spuds with a fork and then bang them into a blindingly hot oven (full blast) for about an hour. Take them out after 40 minutes and test the biggest one with a knife. If they're not ready, test them every 10 minutes thereafter. Once they're cooked through, let them cool for a minute or two so that handling them won't have you in the big house and then cut them in half and scoop out most of the spuddy flesh. The more flesh you leave in, the less crispy and more filling the final product will be. If you'd rather have them covered in melted cheese and bacon bits, don't take too much flesh out.

Now... for arguments sake, let's say we want these for beer accompaniment. Remove most of the flesh and them cut the halves again (effectively cutting the spud skins into quarters). I find a pair of kitchen scissors work well.

Then, using the pastry brush that you only use once in a blue moon, brush the skins, inside and out, with the melted butter. Stick them back into the oven for 5 minutes and hey presto, alternative crisps. All they need now is a dusting of seasoning and a(nother) cold beer.

it takes two
bottles to get past
prep stage and
just when you're
tottering along the
cliffs of starvation,
the oven finally
pays out

take-away at home
chicken fried rice

IF you've been out on the tiles of a Saturday evening, and you suddenly find yourself in a Chinese takeaway at 2am, there is little to compare with the comforting, post-beer, silver platter of chicken fried rice and curry sauce – and maybe even a portion of chips. High on taste intensity and heat, it's messier than a burger but nowhere near kebab dishevelment. I've seen people eating kebabs who've needed hosing down afterwards.

Anyway, when all is said and scoffed, anything tastes good at that time of the day (in that condition) and after a bellyful of amber nectar. An alcohol hunger is one where anything is considered nutrition.

Chicken fried rice had a bad reputation in my house up until a few years ago – and in a way, it still does. Stodgy, wet, saline and greasy, there is nothing surer than you'll find a piece of chicken complete with grizzly fat or a hard bit formed like granite. This is all well and good at 2am, but chicken fried rice sober is a different experience.

As is often the case with fast food, chicken fried rice can be a victim of its own convenience and nowadays the emphasis is firmly set on fast rather than taste. However, visit an establishment which turns these taste tables and you'll find no healthier, more delicious or satisfying a meal.

As I am inclined to do of a Saturday night (when the funds insist that the only tiles I'll be treading are the ones in my kitchen), I once experimented with chicken fried rice and have never looked back. Fresh, fragrant and exceptionally toothsome, Michael's Chicken Fried Rice® is actually a fusion of a whole host of tastes and textures but, like everything else, this can be adjusted for personal sensibilities.

If you want to do the whole Saturday post-pints thing, you can also rustle up the chips and curry sauce, but a bowl of this rice extravaganza should be more then enough. And if you don't fancy any heat, get out of the kitchen (just leave out the chillies).

INGREDIENTS (for two people)

1 clove garlic, chopped
1 tbsp fresh ginger, chopped or grated
1 small red chilli also chopped
2 tbsp vegetable oil
1 tsp sesame oil
2 tbsp soy sauce
2 eggs
227g/8oz pre-cooked long grain rice, chilled
4 spring onions, finely chopped (separate the white bits from the green)
2 large handfuls of frozen peas, thawed and drained
2 large handfuls of chicken (I've discovered this dish is best made with the leftovers from a roast chicken)

handful of chopped coriander
1 baby gem lettuce, shredded
Handful of crushed cashew nuts (I once left these out by mistake and rather liked the change so they aren't absolutely essential)

THE PLAN

Heat the vegetable oil in a wok or large frying pan until it is very hot. Add the garlic and ginger and chilli (if you're using it) and cook for a few seconds, stirring all the time. Next add the cold rice and stir fry for about 2 minutes on a high heat.

Beat the eggs together and add the mixture to the pan. You'll have to work fast at this stage unless you want scrambled eggs so stir fry quickly until the eggs have set – this shouldn't take any more than a few seconds.

as I am inclined to do of a Saturday night (when the funds insist that the only tiles I'll be treading are the ones in my kitchen), I once experimented with chicken fried rice and have never looked back.

_____

Add the peas, chicken, spring onions (white bits), stir around again and then drip in some soy and the sesame oil. At this stage it should start to smell heavenly.

Give it another 30 seconds at the end of cooking mix in the coriander, baby gem, green spring onions and the nuts. Check the seasoning and you're there.

Hot or cold, this is super tucker. You'll feel like Ken Holm and so long as you don't over cook it, this will be aeons away from the greasy fare you'd receive on a Saturday night.

Instead of the chicken, you could do cubes of ham or even prawns – or maybe even a combination of all three, though I haven't tried that one out yet. No doubt I'll have a few some Saturday night and the Michael's Special Fried Combo® will be born.

spiky comfort food
chilli con carne

YOU know sometimes you hear cooks talking about wearing rubber gloves when handling hot chilli peppers? I used to think this was an overly protective precaution and only really necessary if you were having a child (or a simpleton) do the chopping – in case they picked their nose or rubbed an eye. That is, until recently...

I was chopping a Scotch Bonnet at the time (well above average on the heat scale) and I wasn't wearing any gloves, although I was also taking care not to rub or touch any delicate parts of my anatomy. The chilli was halved, de-seeded and finely chopped and everything was going swimmingly. I then tasted a seed to check to see how much I'd be using in my chilli con carne. It was hot – damn hot – so I reckoned I'd only need about half.

I continued cooking for a few moments until I noticed the tips of my fingers beginning to ache and burn. I was befuddled until I finally cottoned on to what had happened. Somehow, the juice from the chilli had penetrated my skin and was burning my fingers on the inside. I scrutinized my fingertips and then washed my hands but to no avail, there was nothing to wash off and the agony was happening under the skin. I dread to think how bad the pain would have been if I'd changed a contact lens or something.

A strange phenomenon, chilli peppers are the marmite of the fruit world (that's right they're fruits), you either love them or hate them – though I reckon some people only think they don't like them. Measured on the Scoville scale, chillies range from the mild and sweet bell pepper (0 units) that we all know and love up to the nuclear meltdown of the naga jolokia (1,000,000 units approx), which could literally, as Dirty Harry would say, "Blow your head clean off, punk." But for most dishes you don't have to use rocket fuel chillies.

There are many and wondrous ways of using these little taste bombs, although making a good olde fashioned chilli con carne takes some beating. It's a bit of a mission, but I tend to make it when we're having friends around and it always goes down a bomb. I don't like it kicking like a donkey either; just with a little nippy tang.

INGREDIENTS

2 red chillies (de-seeded and chopped), the variety is up to you, but birdeyes work well
1 dessert spoon of chilli powder (hot or mild, you choose)
1 teaspoon of cumin seeds
2 tins of tomatoes
2 tins of kidney beans (drained)
olive oil
Splash of Worchester sauce
2 onions
2 cloves of garlic

half a beef Oxo cube
half a jar of sun-dried tomato paste (not the pesto one), or 2 tbsp of tomato puree
500g or roughly a pound of steak mince
salt and pepper
Lime wedges (to serve)

THE PLAN

First, toast your cumin seeds in a dry frying pan for a few minutes. You just want to heat them through really, so when they start to smell sensational, they're done. Pound them in a mortar and pestle and set aside.

Finely chop the onion and garlic and then fry in some olive oil in a heavy based pan, on a lowish heat until they're soft. Toss in the chilli powder, chopped chillies and cumin and stir about. Turn your heat up and fling in the mince, the crumbled Oxo cube and a pinch of salt and some pepper and brown this off.

Then add the half jar of sun-dried tomato paste, the two cans of tomatoes, the Worchester and a dash of water.

Bring this up to a gentle simmer and then cover and let it bubble away for at least an hour. Stir every 15 minutes or so to make sure it doesn't dry up. If it looks a little dry, add another dash of water. Then 10 minutes before the end, dump in the kidney beans. Check the seasoning at the end and you're done. Mince with spices always tastes better the next day, so if you make this on a Sunday try it with a baked potato on a Monday night and a sprinkling of cheese.

Alternatively, you could have it with rice, spilt over tortilla chips with melted cheese; wrapped it in wraps with some sour cream like a burrito; with chips or a side salad; over crusty bread with more cheese, or simply on its own, in a big bowl with a big spoon and a big smile on your face.

It's great telly food too, especially when you slitter it all over the sofa and the missus goes mad.

THERE'S something about pizza on a Saturday night which makes ultimate food sense. I'm not sure what it is exactly.

Maybe it's the unpretentious nature of the slice in hand or the way it's just made for sharing. Or maybe it's just that it's super-tasty, no-nonsense and handy.

It's hard to beat a good pizza delivered by the man in the van but with a bit of effort it's amazing what you can achieve at home.

After a bit of practice, making a pizza from scratch is seriously tasty. Unfortunately, this is probably the ultimate effort for a Saturday night and I must admit, it's mostly beyond me except on special occasions.   Mixing the dough, kneading, proving, waiting, rolling, toppings, baking... it all takes a lot of time. The upside to that of course, is that it gives you plenty of time to slake your thirst – which, if it's like mine, goes haywire on a Saturday night.

Making your own dough is the best way for the perfect pizza. I use a certain Mr Oliver's recipe from the 'Jamie's Italy' book, and to date, I have yet to make a mess of it. The step by step instructions are second to none. It's also the basic recipe for his bread – which you can bake with any left over dough.

You could also go down the pre-prepared packet pizza mix, although in terms of effort versus reward, you're almost better going the whole hog and starting from scratch. You still have to mix, knead and prove.

Similarly, if you're glued to the sofa, a frozen pizza is a good emergency substitute but again, these are invariably and ultimately let downs.

Over the years, I've pretty much tried to pizza everything from French sticks to crumpets – I even tried potato bread once, which didn't really work. That said, a half a soda farl works quite well for an Irish version.

One of the bestest successes in recent times has been my Mexican pizzas which come with no mixing, kneading or anything remotely resembling work.

For the pizza base, use a single tortilla wrap. Placed on some tin foil, followed by the sauce and then the toppings and blasted in a blindingly hot oven for four minutes and it's done. How easy is that?

In fact, the hardest part will be making your tomato sauce. The pizza is quick, infinitely sharable and very, very delicious. Plus the thin base lets the toppings shine through.

The only thing you have to have right is the tomato sauce and everything else normally falls into place. The sauce base has to be deep, slightly sweet and nicely herby. Buy the most expensive can of tomatoes you can find and you can't go wrong.

INGREDIENTS (for the TOMATO SAUCE)

1 can of tomatoes
1 clove garlic, finely sliced
pinch of sugar

olive oil
knob of butter
half tsp of dried oregano
seasoning

THE PLAN

Add a glug of olive oil to a sauce pan and throw in the garlic. You just want to show it to the heat, so when it starts to sizzle give it ten seconds and then add the can of tomatoes. Turn the heat down to its lowest setting, fling in the oregano a big pinch of sugar and stir it about. You want to let this bubble away slowly until it has reached a spreadable sauce consistency – it'll take anything from 15 to 30 minutes. Don't be tempted to break up the tomatoes, the cooking will do that. If you break them up early the seeds will make the sauce slightly bitter. Just give it odd gentle stir to make sure it doesn't stick and burn.

When you think it's thick enough (this is basically when all the water has evaporated away), drop in the knob of butter, stir about and taste for seasoning. When you're topping up the pizza – especially this tortilla kind – less is more. If you overload it, it'll be soggy and floppy. But don't worry, if you make a mess of the first one, just have another. I can easily put away three of these mehico pizzas (in-between beers) on a Saturday night.

the big kahuna
home made burgers

I LOVE burgers. Big, hefty, meaty sandwiches, oozing with mayo, relish and melting cheese, a few shards of onion and maybe a slice of crisped-up bacon – oh and a handful of chips on the side – the messier the better.

Generally we know the ubiquitous burger as the epitome of fast food. McDonalds, Burger King and America in general are forever championing the hamburger, as they call it, as big taste for the (big) man on the run. Big Macs, Whoppers or Whopping Macs – I've tried them all at one time or another – the impressionable clown that I am. I'm such a sucker for advertising (I'm lovin' it).

These days, I often seem to find myself in one of the international burger joints when I'm away with the lads for whatever reason. It's the handiness aspect, I suppose and the fact that these establishments aren't overly serious – perfect for a gaggle of half-sozzled football supporters.

And yet, I more often than not think that take-away burgers tend to disappoint – unless you're completely sozzled. They're just so insipid. The idea is often right, but the end product never lives up to the hype.

The easy option, if you want to have your burger and eat it, is to buy a steak burger from a reputable butcher. However, if you want ultra-taste, there's only one route you can go down and that's the good-olde, home-made way.

I find myself crafting some home-made Kahunas if we're having a party or sometimes even after a night out. They're informal, satisfying and plus you can eat with your hands without the need for knives and forks and place mats etc. Plus, all the prep can be done ahead of time too, so all you have to worry about is cooking off the burgers and stacking them on the buns with whatever takes your fancy.

The other great thing about burgers is that you can tailor them to suit your own particular tastes. For example, if you like chillies then bang a load of those in. If you don't, don't.

Michael's Big Kahuna won't suit everyone's tastes, but this Michael happens to think they are beyond great. Fresher, more succulent and very, very fulfilling, it's the method that counts, and once you get the hang of them, you can vary the bits and pieces to suit. The following list if for four rather big, Big Kahunas.

Big Macs, Whoppers or Whopping Macs – I've tried them all at one time or another – the impressionable clown that I am. I'm such a sucker for advertising (I'm lovin' it).

INGREDIENTS

1lb or roughly 500g of steak mince
2 free range egg yolks
big handful of breadcrumbs
1 onion, (finely chopped and softened in butter with a touch of seasoning)
big pinch of cumin seeds
heaped tsp of coriander seeds
handful of grated parmesan

1 birdseye chilli pepper (finely chopped)
heaped tsp of Dijon or whole grain mustard
oil for frying
salt and pepper

THE PLAN

First pound your cumin and coriander with a few peppercorns and some sea salt. Then toss all the burger ingredients with one of the handfuls of breadcrumbs into a big mixing bowl and get your hands in to mix is all up. If you're like me, this will be messy, but slightly therapeutic.

Divide into four and shape out the burgers. I find that the thinner you can make them at this stage the better, because once they hit the pan they always tend to thicken up a bit. Try to make them about half a centimetre thick.

Once you've got your burgers shaped out, leave them to chill in the fridge for an hour. This makes them hold together more and they're less likely to come apart when your add heat to the equation.

After that, all you have to do is fry them up and I normally do this on a griddle pan with a little touch of oil. Have it at a fairly high heat and all you have to do is watch you don't move them about too much, otherwise they break up and revert back to their mince state. About four to five minutes on each side should do the trick, but about one minute before the end, I add the cheese to the tops of the burger – it gets a better chance to melt this way.

TO SERVE

I won't insult your intelligence by telling you how to assemble your burgers but I will say that I normally lightly toast the buns. You can use whatever cheese you like but I reckon bog standard pre-wrapped cheese slices take some beating.

I also normally add a few sliced gherkins, some sliced raw red onions, mayo AND tomato ketchup, a leaf or two of iceberg lettuce and some strips of streaky bacon.

I tend to veer away from tomatoes as these bad boys normally make their way onto my shirt.

Then all you need are some hot chips and bada-bing! you're Samuel L Jackson in Pulp Fiction. "This IS mighty a tasty burger."

four... adventures in cheese

better than marilyn
steak roquefort

I USED to eat Steak Roquefort about once a month when I lived in Corsica. U Spuntinu, a tiny restaurant in the hilly town of Corte had many excellent *plats*, but this one earned a special place in my heart because it was the first time I'd ever encountered the combination (and my arteries are probably still struggling).

Always an ardent blue cheese fan – though soapy Danish Blues and Stiltons pale into insignificance compared with this – I also first tasted Roquefort during that year in the Med and it's a taste I often revisit, though not as often as I'd like.

Tangy, salty, moist and deliciously robust, for me, this sheep's milk cheese tastes as though you would imagine blue cheese should.

According to legend, Roquefort was first discovered when a young man, probably a shepherd, was sitting outside his cave eating his lunch. Upon seeing a beautiful mademoiselle off in the distance, he bundled all his lunchables into the cave and set off posthaste to accost said damsel. When he returned some months later (he must have been busy), his cheese has been magically transformed into the classic blue by mould in the cave, Penicillium roqueforti.

More recently, Roquefort also has the distinction of being the first recipient of France's Appellation d'Origine Contrôlée (controlled term of origin) in 1925 when regulations controlling its production and naming was first defined. (The origins of AOC date back to the 15th century, when Roquefort was regulated by a parliamentary decree).

All I know is: It tastes good – too good in fact.

There are loads of things you can do with Roquefort, though personally, I never have it in the house long enough to think about recipes. For a weekend lunch, I eat it thinly sliced with a few grapes or an apple and a lump of crusty bread. Or in salad format, crumbled over some rocket with walnuts and honey, it's always delicious.

Most often I take little nips of the cheese as I'm grazing on a Saturday night in between a beer or two or a glass of red wine.

Steak Roquefort, as they say in U Spuntinu is hard to whack. Not for the faint of heart, this is a dish you'll have to limit yourself eating, although if you've already tried it, you'll know what I mean.

INGREDIENTS

knob of butter
dash of olive oil
two steaks of your choice
salt and pepper
tablespoon of brandy
200 ml of double cream
90g of Roquefort
big pinch of chopped parsley

THE PLAN

Add the oil and butter to a frying pan and place on a high heat (second highest set-

ting). Season the steaks on both sides, and once the butter's foaming and it's good and hot, add the steaks to the pan. Give them at least a minute on either side, turn the heat down a notch and continue to cook to your liking (2 to 3 minutes for medium and 4 to 5 minutes for well done although the precise times will depend on the thickness of the steaks).

Once the steaks are done, remove from the pan, turn up the heat and add the brandy. Stir and scrape with a wooden spoon to dislodge all the lovely caramelised bits, turn the heat down and add the cream. Bring to a simmer and cook until thickened slightly (until it coats the back of a spoon). Crumble in the cheese, stir until melted and then add the parsley.

Pour the sauce over the steaks and serve with some simple salad leaves. You'll also want some bread for mopping.

If Marilyn Monroe herself walked into the room when I was eating this dish, I'd clean the plate before I introduced myself.

According to legend, Roquefort was first discovered when a young man, probably a shepherd, was sitting outside his cave eating his lunch. Upon seeing a beautiful mademoiselle off in the distance, he bundled all his lunchables into the cave and set off post-haste to accost said damsel. When he returned some months later (he must have been busy), his cheese has been magically transformed into the classic blue by mould in the cave, *Penicillium roqueforti*.

run, rarebit, run
irish rarebit

I HAVE a lot of time for Smithwick's, too much in fact. Although in fairness, I could probably say that about beer in general.

The world's oldest and most widely consumed alcoholic beverage, beer is the third most popular drink on the planet after water and tea. And sometimes I feel duty bound to maintain this trend.

Similarly, Smithwick's is Ireland's oldest brewery, founded by John Smithwick in 1710 at the St Francis Abbey Brewery in Kilkenny, later known as 'Smithwicks Brewery'. Situated on the site of a Franciscan abbey, monks had also brewed there since the 14th century, no doubt shaving their heads on a regular basis, arguing about football from time to time and considering ordering lamb bhunas – after having had a few. This also, is a trend I like to perpetuate – minus the shaving of the head, of course.

Ruby red and infinitely drinkable, Smithwick's is a wondrous creation and lends itself to all manner of salty snacking of a weekend. It also goes particularly well in a beef stew, but that's a story for another time.

I have just recently discovered that this Irish ale also lends itself particularly well to that Rolls Royce of cheese sarnies, Welsh Rarebit.

Fashioning one once I had no dark ale as the quintessential recipe demanded and so I substituted the dark brew with Smithwick's. You might say the cheesy snack then became Irish Rarebit.

Similar to a croque monsieur (*see page 40 for recipe*), rarebit is a rich little snack and not something you could have everyday. As with a bog-standard cheese sandwich you can add everything from ham to chicken to Branston pickle but I like the simplicity of the stripped back version.

see page 40 for recipe

The world's oldest and most widely consumed alcoholic beverage, beer is the third most popular drink on the planet after water and tea. And sometimes I feel duty bound to maintain this trend.

INGREDIENTS (FOR ONE)

1 piece of toast
heaped teaspoon of plain flour
big knob of butter
handful of strong cheddar cheese (about 70-100g)
100 ml (good dash) of Smithwick's
salt and pepper
cayenne pepper
Worcestershire sauce

THE PLAN

Start of by lightly toasting the bread. As this is happening, add the knob of butter to the pan, melt and then add the flour. Cook on a medium heat for two minutes and then add the Smithwick's. Stir around until the alcohol has burned off (you can't smell it anymore) then add the cheese, turn the heat way down low and slowly stir and melt until the cheese has been incorporated. Season with salt and pepper, spoon the cheesy mixture over the bread – don't be afraid to be generous – and blast under a hot grill for about 30 seconds or until bubbling and irresistible.

Remove from the oven, add a splash of Worcestershire and a dusting of cayenne and that's it. Irish Rarebit.

OK, so this is basically fancy cheese on toast, but I guarantee you won't be complaining when you're eating it.

Also, you might wonder at the relatively small amount of Smithwick's that goes into the recipe. However, I have discovered a cunning way around this potential wastage. Before you start the cooking process, measure out the 100 ml that you will require, pour the rest into a glass and consume at your leisure.

Shaving your head is optional.

can you hear me Ben Gunn?
for the love of cheese

ONE of my abiding memories of Treasure Island is poor Ben Gunn. Action, intrigue and Long John Silver aside, I had a soft spot the half-insane ex-pirate because he had forgotten what cheese tasted like. No wonder he wasn't wise. He might as well have been slipped the Black Spot!

The first time I read the Robert Louis Stevenson masterpiece as a child, I wondered what I'd forget the taste of, if I was ever cast aside by my pirate buddies (for scoffing all the hard tack or drinking all the rum). I was pretty sure however, it wouldn't be cheese.

These days I have to limit the amount of cheese I eat; I will freely admit, I'm pretty addicted. Whether it's on its own out of the fridge for a snack on the run, grated over a home-made bolognese or blue and dripping with honey – various cheeses have a veritable myriad of uses. In fact, it's pretty difficult to imagine life without cheese and maybe that was Ben's problem.

I remember one Friday afternoon I was planning making pizza and I was bemoaning a certain local supermarket's lack of mozzarella to a work colleague. "Can you believe all they have is cheddar cheese?" I ranted.

"What other kind of cheese can you get?" came the reply.

Now, I'm not saying there's anything wrong with cheddar cheese and there are many fine examples lining our supermarket shelves – Extra Mature Irish Cheddar from Fivemiletown Creamery is an especially great product and right on our doorstep to boot. What I can't understand is stocking 15 different kinds of cheddar and nothing else. Although by the same token, if your clientele only know about cheddar, you can't shoulder all the blame. Some local restaurants have also started suggesting a cheese-board as an after dinner snack, in place of the ubiquitous apple pies and pavlova. And why not, especially since Fivemiletown is only over the hill.

One of life's great pleasures, as far as I'm concerned, is melting a shard of something powerful, creamy and unctuous on your tongue before washing the lot down with something robust, juicy and red. Even breathing takes on new meaning after that. I'm going all misty-eyed just thinking about it.

made the mistake of tasting some. Fresh and strong and uncommonly good (as Mr Kipling might say) Corleggy Goat's Cheese is apparently produced on the hilly pastures, on the banks of the River Erne.

Anyway, I took my bounty home and stored it, as suggested in the bottom of the fridge. The lady also suggested at the time that the cheese would mature all the way to Christmas. So, I thought, that's just what I'll do. The things is: This cheese is killing me at the moment. Every time I open the fridge a waft of cheesy goodness brushes my nostrils and I consider, for the umpteenth time (that day), knocking off a tranche there and then and snaffling it, eyes rolling. I have purposely avoided buying some green grapes and crusty bread (which I reckon would bring the cheese onto another level of greatness) so that temptation won't become too much.

I don't know what I'm waiting for really. Maybe it's a partner in cheese, someone to share the bounty with (since the missus can't have the smell, never mind the taste).

Can you hear me Ben Gunn?

Only our finest cheddars are selected to become Oakwood after maturing for up to 6 months. Our oak logs are sustainably foraged from the local Forest of Caledon and then slowly smouldered to release rich plumes of smoke that impart a gentle smoky flavour and robust aroma.

The reason I mention it, cheese that is, is that I recently purloined an individual goats cheese from a lady at a farmer's market at An Creggan.

I wasn't after cheese at all but

AS a nipper, I recall scoffing at the idea of cheesecake; it didn't make sense. Cakes were crumbly things old people ate with tea (young people slurped in custard), whereas cheese was something you had on your sandwiches or pizzas – never the twain should meet. Everyone knew their place in my infantile world.

Until I tasted one, that is.

Even now, it's hard to think of a better dessert than a well-prepared and perfectly balanced cheese cake. If I'm honest, I don't really make too many desserts, unless it's for a special occasion – except cheesecakes.

The right proportion of crunchy biscuit to cheesy cream is such a little detail but so important at the same time and when you bite into the cream followed by the base, something happens, something special; it makes ultimate pudding sense. If ever textures made a difference to enjoying food, then this is it. Tastes are paramount of course, as they always are, but it is a strange and yet undeniable fact that you can have a bland cheesecake and still enjoy it.

I would never have dreamt of tasting Bailey's cheesecake either until a friend introduced me to the same. I'm not a fan of sickly Bailey's on ice and I would never have dreamt it might work in cheese cake format. It does though and how it does. Just the essence of the Baileys shines through making every mouthful something of a culinary orgasm.

I think if I had to pick just one cheese cake however, the one that I never tire of eating, it would to be the classic strawberry cake. Sweet, unctuous and gratifying for the inner child, more often than not I can hardly stop making a glutton of myself. Thanks the Lord for Andrews.

The best news is: A great cheesecake is within everyone cook's grasp – even for a first timer. So long as you have the proper equipment (a cake tin with a removable bottom), it's almost impossible to mess it up – almost. I've even made individual cheese cakes in those disposable tin cake tins, but nothing beats the wow-factor of a big cake out of the tin.

The following recipe is for quick strawberry cheese cake and I can't recommend this one highly enough. I did say 'quick' right enough, but it does need chilling in the fridge over night. It's great if you're having people over for dinner because it can be done the night before.

INGREDIENTS

300g of biscuits (the oatier the better, but even bog standard digestives work well, as do Hobnobs)
120g of real butter
2 drops of vanilla extract
80g of icing sugar (or caster sugar at a pinch)
small pot of double cream (280ml)
600g of mascarpone (or any soft cream cheese)
1 large punnet of strawberries, hulled and sliced (leave the smallest ones whole)

Put the biscuits into a sandwich bag and crush with a rolling pin or your fist. Go gently here otherwise the bag will burst and you'll be sweeping up crumbs. Also, you might want to do this in two batches if the bags are small.

Melt the butter in a small pan and when it starts to foam, dump in the crushed biscuits and mix thoroughly. It should start to smell divine.

Now line your cake tin. For this amount of ingredients it has to be around 23 cm in diameter. Butter and line the tin with baking parchment first – this is a bit of a hanlin' the first time around but you soon get the hang of it. In fact I normally get the missus to do it for me.

Now apply the biscuit base, firming down slightly along the sides, making as even a layer as possible. IMPORTANT: Don't firm down to hard, otherwise the base will be too hard when you come to cut into it – I've made this mistake more than once. When you're happy, put it into the fridge for at least an hour to set.

In a large mixing bowl, combine the mascarpone and the icing sugar and beat well until smooth. Don't panic about lumps, just give it more elbow grease and it'll be fine. That done, tip in the cream and again, mix thoroughly. Add the drops of vanilla extract and give it one more mix for luck.

Spoon the cheese mix into the biscuit base, smoothing as you go. When it's all in, smooth the top with the back of a spoon and bang it in the fridge for its overnight chillout.

Next day to get it out of the cake tin or mould, you're kind of one your own, since instructions will only go so far. I normally allow the cake to come to room temperature for about an hour or so and then set it on a can of beans and gradually slip the cake tin's sides down – with extreme care.

Slide it onto a large flat plate, removing the parchment. At this stage I'm normally holding my breath I'm so close.

All you have to do now is pile on the slices strawberries, higgledy-piggledy, dust with a little more icing sugar and you're done.

If you can remember, take a picture, it'll be beautiful enough.

AS I've never been there (or even had much of an inclination to go), I reckon I might have a kind of skewed opinion of the country, what with all the international 'incidents' and what-have-you. Consequently, I might not be the most enthusiastic person for all things American – apart from Tom and Jerry – oh, and westerns.

And yet, I have to admit that from a distance, America isn't without it's taste. I'm thinking of fried chicken, fresh jambalaya, creamy chowders, unctuous apple pies, Boston baked beans, potent buffalo wings, cheese burgers – grub which is natural, unpretentious and with enough calorific content to launch a space shuttle.

Say what you like about their foreign policy, the yanks certainly know how to light their barbecues – not that you could tell by the look of them or anything. And yet, when I think of it again, most of the foods which spring to mind are all of European descent. And so is macaroni cheese.

A firm favourite on the far side of the pond, macaroni cheese (or mac and cheese, as they like to call it) is an adulteration of French and Italian cuisines, the macaroni obviously pasta and the sauce with more than a faint echo of the French Mornay.

Macaroni cheese is not, by any stretch of an over-active imagination, a very healthy dish – unless of course you have just a small portion. The combination of cheese, butter, bread, flour, and pasta ticks only one box: Arbuckle√. The bad news is that macaroni cheese is hard to beat for comfort food and holding a fresh bake makes you feel like you've just morphed into a pillow. Eating a whole bowl makes you feel like a very satisfied but stuffed pillow.

The good news is that there is another kind of macaroni cheese; one which doesn't contain the necessary kilojoules to power a small African country and one which also contains all the vegetables the original doesn't – which is never a bad thing – five a day and all that. No sacrifice in taste, however.

This version of the American classic is also a lot lighter and fresher. Gone is the heavy and thick, Mornay sauce only to be replaced by a slighter, dreamier, cream sauce. Another plus point for this particular dish is that it literally couldn't be easier. The hardest bit will be cooking the pasta.

INGREDIENTS (feeds 4)

350g of macaroni (or if you can't get macaroni, just use any small shaped pasta)
500 ml or roughly 1 pint of single cream
4 or 5 (depending on size) large ripe tomatoes (tip: sweet is neat!)
4 sun dried tomatoes (the ones in the oil)
2/3 anchovy fillets
pinch pf fresh nutmeg
1 clove of garlic
1 handfuls of breadcrumbs

2 big handfuls of freshly grated parmesan (is there any other kind)
1 egg
handful of grated mozzarella
handful of fresh basil
big knob of butter
salt and pepper

THE PLAN

As I say, this couldn't be easier. Set your oven to warming to 190°C and while that is happening cook the macaroni to the packet instructions. Fling all your ingredients except the cream, breadcrumbs, one handful of the parmesan and the mozzarella into a blender and blend until smooth. Normally I start with just the tomatoes and the garlic. For some reason liquidising the vegetables is an immensely gratifying experience.

After you've blended the veggie cheese mix, add the cream and the egg and give it another wiz.

When the pasta is cooked drain and dump into a large baking dish. Add the creamy mixture and stir through the mozzarella. Taste and season (if necessary) at this stage and then top with the remaining breadcrumbs and parmesan. Dot with the butter and bang it in the pre-heated oven. That's it.

Cook for 10 to 15 minutes or until the top is golden and irresistible and then scoff without delay. A chuck of garlic bread would go well here and possibly some dry white wine.

"America, America..."

five... giving your taste-buds the boot... Italy... get it?... the boot?... ahh...

snacking italian style
fraghetti

WHAT is the tastiest snack in the world? No doubt this is decided the world over on a daily basis in terms of personal relish, disposition and environment.

One man's passion is another man's random detritus, after all. But for a moment, suspend disbelief and imagine there is such a thing as the World Championships for The Tastiest Snack In The World®

Who would win? I think I have a contender.

During a recent trip to Italy I came into contact with a new twist on spaghetti, one I am surprised I have never noticed before, especially since it has turned out to be such a revelation.

Since I've returned home I find myself making it at every opportunity. If you come to the house, I have to make it for you. If I'm having a beer I have to make it. If it's raining outside, I'll have to make it. I'm not entirely sure what makes it so great, but I simply cannot get enough of Fried Spaghetti.

I understand this may sound like a bit of a contradiction in culinary terms but fried spaghetti or spaghetti fritters or whatever it's called in Italy is better than you can imagine it to be.

Actually for the purpose of this discussion, we will now refer to the fried spaghetti as Fraghetti. So, how do you make it?

INGREDIENTS

handful of normal, bog-standard spaghetti or tagliatelle
1 egg
1 clove of garlic (finely sliced)
half a chilli pepper (finely chopped)
1 tomato, deseeded and finely chopped
handful of grated parmesan (forget about the pre-grated stuff it's rank)
handful of chopped fresh herbs any variety with big leaves
a good glug of olive oil

THE PLAN

Well, all you have to do – and this literally couldn't be simpler is, boil up your small handful of spaghetti as you normally would according to the packet instructions – but break in two first. While that's happening, crack the egg into a bowl and add the chopped clove of garlic, parmesan, chilli pepper and a handful of whatever fresh herbs you can get your hands on and mix well. Herbwise, I have so far tried flat leaf parsley and basil and even a combination of both and they work supremely well.

Once your spaghetti is cooked through, let it go beyond al dente for best results, drain and run under cold water to cool through. When that's done, season the eggy mixture (adding salt too soon to eggs makes them go all watery) and then dump the spaghetti into the mix. Mix this all about and you're almost there.

Heat the olive oil in a frying pan and then, using a fork, pick up a little load and dump into the pan. I haven't timed it, but this should take any more than a few minutes either side but ideally, the spaghetti fritter should be golden and crispy on the outside and moist and succulent inside. You can make them as big or as little as you like, but once you've done a few you'll soon decide how you like them.

When it's cooked, stick it on a bit of kitchen paper to drain. Add a sprinkling of sea salt and enjoy.

I am not kidding when I say that this has changed my snacking life for ever more. Even just thinking about it means I'm going to have to have it this evening. One of these and a beer is sheer bliss.

Just in case you were wondering, Spaghetti is the plural form of the Italian word spaghetto, which is a diminutive of "spago," meaning "thin string" or "twine". The word "spaghetti" can be literally translated as "little strings."

Little strings of lethalness.

ferry risotto
in a bow

pesto greeno
green pesto

IT is little known fact that rubbing a crushed basil leaf on your skin will repel mosquitoes – not that we get too many of those little buggers in this part of the world – but with the environment going down the toilet, there's plenty of time yet.

Another fascinating food factoid is that adding a few drops of basil's essential oil onto a cloth and inhaling is said to relieve mental fatigue. And here was me thinking it only tasted good.

Native to India, the Middle East and some Pacific islands, basil has been cultivated and cherished since man first realised that tasty food was better. Steeped in lore, the plant's common name is believed to be a derivative of Basilikon phuton (Greek for kingly herb) and it was said to have grown around Christ's tomb after the resurrection. And yet, there is also some question as to the sanctity of basil and both the Romans and the Greeks maintained that people should, when sowing the seeds, curse to ensure germination. Although, in Europe, it was also held to be a remedy against witches. Strange.

There are plethoric variations of the same plant, from 'Sacred Basil' to 'Bush Basil' but the one we are most familiar with is 'Sweet Basil' which hails from Genoa in the north of Italy – hence it's local name, Genovese. Sweet basil has, as everyone knows, a particular affinity with both garlic and tomatoes and is used extensively throughout Italian cuisine. Basil is one of the few herbs to decrease in flavour when cooked, thus the unique flavour of torn leaves is added at the end of the cooking for maximum effect. Although the plant does not bond well with strong meats such as venison, basil makes an interesting accompanying stuffing for chicken.

Happy as Larry on a kitchen windowsill the only thing to remember is do not over water basil, and when you do water, do so in the middle of the day. Basil hates to go to bed wet.

One of the true joys of Basil I find, is making fresh pesto sauce. For some reason this makes me feel sort of guiltily decadent, since you have to use so much of it. But the resulting sauce is so delicious, it's virtually addictive.

For this recipe, I've left the amounts of ingredients purposely imprecise. It's the method that's important and if you use fresh ingredients, you'll never go too far wrong.

INGREDIENTS

small handful of pine nuts (I've also used almonds and walnuts)
2 big handfuls of basil leaves
1 clove of garlic
2 handfuls of freshly grated parmesan
Olive oil

Toast up your pine nuts in a dry frying pan. Really, you just want to warm these through without adding too much colour. When this is happening, bash up the garlic in a mortar and pestle with a pinch of sea salt. Then add the pine nuts and give this a real good hammering. Fling in the basil and pound mercilessly. It should start to smell like you've died and gone to nasal heaven.

When you have the mixture in a paste of sorts, scrap it out into a bowl. Add about two or three tablespoons of the oil to loosen it up and then add the cheese. Stir this up good and well and, if you need to, add more oil. You want a paste-like consistency. Not exactly runny but almost – like thick porridge. If you think it's a little too runny, just add more parmesan but once you've tried it a few times, you'll soon get the hang of it. Season well and tah-dah!

Add to freshly cooked pasta, cover pork chops, chicken breasts, or even just spread onto toast with some grated cheese – this is heavenly stuff.

Pesto will keep in a sealed container in the fridge for up to a week. Good luck with that.

if it's good enough for garfield...
lasagne

IT seems to me that Italy is where it's at when it comes to taste. There are no airs and graces with Italian food. It just good, earthy, natural, traditional stuff, products like olive oil, mozzarella and cured meats, things which celebrate quality above pretension. Sometimes I think we can be overly elaborate with recipes and ways of cooking.

For as far back as I can remember, lasagne has been a big part of my life. Garfield was mad about it and if it was good enough for him, it was good enough for me. Often called Lasagne al forno, meaning "Lasagne in the oven", lasagne is, in my humble opinion, one of the great triumphs of the human race. Forget the wheel or flying or missions to the moon, or traffic wardens, lasagne is the peak of civilisation – in culinary terms at least. It's also a contradiction in culinary terms. It's so simple and yet such a mission, messy yet organised, small yet filling – but above all else, lasagne is decadence. Personally, if I'm eating lasagne I want it to be as tasty as possible, so if that means it'll be high on calories, then so be it. But it isn't everyday I'm going to be eating it either – more's the pity.

Traditionally and most often made with alternating layers of tomato sauce, béchamel, cheese and sheets of pasta, lasagne is made the world over in a multitude of ways. The one I'm about to show you is, as far as I have ever tasted, the best. But be clear about it, this is off the scale as far as fat is concerned. One portion is probably about 1,000 calories but when you taste it, it's like a drug and you'll have to keep coming back for more. Aeons away from the frozen junk in supermarkets, this is the stuff I'd order for my last meal.

INGREDIENTS (For the meat sauce)

tbsp of butter
glug of olive oil
3 celery stalks, finely diced
unsmoked pancetta, chopped (streaky bacon will do)
2 onions roughly chopped
500g steak mince
3 cloves garlic, chopped
500g/chopped tomatoes
two glasses of red wine (try and get Italian stuff. And it's one for you and one for the recipe)
2 bay leaves
1 beef stock cube
loads of fresh oregano, basil and parsley (you should be able to find the basil and parsley fresh and if you have to substitute the fresh oregano with a teaspoon of the dried variety).
black pepper
2 tbsp tomato purée

2tsp plain flour
Packet of lasagne sheets
80g grated parmesan cheese and the same of grated mozzarella
For the béchamel sauce
250ml full-fat milk
1 onion
2 cloves
bay leaf
50g butter
60 plain flour
150ml single cream

THE PLAN

Start frying the bacon in butter and a glug of olive oil to get it started then after a minute of two add the onions and celery. Cook gently until the onion softens and the bacon starts to brown.

Tip in the mince and garlic and cook until the beef has browned. This should take about 5 or 6 minutes. Then add the passata/chopped tomatoes, wine, herbs and seasoning, stock cube, tomato purée and bay leaf. Simmer at a low heat uncovered for at least 40 minutes, stirring every so often.

Towards the end of the cooking, add about a tablespoon of plain flour. This will thicken the sauce and emulsify the oils.

Meanwhile, prepare the béchamel sauce. Put the milk, cloves, onion and bay leaf into a small pan and heat gently until the milk simmers. Remove the bay leaf, onion and cloves and bin them.

Melt the butter over low heat, then add the flour and stir to form a paste. Cook over a low heat for 2 minutes.

When this is done, slowly pour in the heated milk, whilst whisking. Bring to a simmer, stirring continuously to form a thick sauce. Once simmering, add the cream and heat until it nearly simmers again. Remove from heat and season. (Stir in an egg yolk here for maximum decadence).

Preheat the oven to 200°C.

Spread a layer of meat sauce on the bottom of a lasagne dish. Cover with dried lasagne sheets. Spread these with a layer of the béchamel sauce, then sprinkle with grated cheeses. Repeat these layers three or four times, finishing with the parmesan. Top with some dried oregano and black pepper then place in the oven to heat through and brown for about 20-30 minutes.

Perfect with a big gutsy red wine, a side salad and some crusty bread, this Italian speciality is perfect all year round, but on the first day that you can eat outside after the bleakness of winter, it's unbeatable.

lasagne is, in my humble opinion, one of the great triumphs of the human race. Forget the wheel or flying or missions to the moon, or traffic wardens, lasagne is the peak of civilisation – in culinary terms at least.

when nothing else will do...
chicken and pea risotto

ONCE upon a time, I took a notion of making some risotto and then wished I hadn't.

Being in receipt of a huge amount of top quality home-made chicken stock (*see page 135 for chicken broth recipe*), I reckoned the best way to use it up would be a simple risotto with some peas and chicken chunks. I could envisage it all perfectly: Oozing parmesan loveliness in a big bowl with a few thyme flowers and maybe a drizzle of cream – I couldn't wait to get stuck in.

So I pulled out all the ingredients and chopped up some onions and celery, whistling as I worked. But the moment I reached for the rice, the whistling stopped. I realised I didn't have any.

What I should have said was, "Oh well, it's not to be," and stuck a frozen pizza in the oven for supper. But since I had everything underway, and the thought of the chicken stock in the fridge going to waste, I jumped into the car and headed for town. But could I find anywhere that sells risotto rice?

Ten different types of pasta shapes (I counted them in one shop) and acres of different brands of long grain rice, there wasn't a single grain to be had of risotto. I could understand it if I was looking for vintage sturgeon caviar or dodo eggs or duck-billed platypus eye lashes but all I wanted was rice.

I tried three different places until I finally gave up, went home, had a cheese and pickled onion sandwich and hoped the chicken stock would last another day.

Marks and Spencers came to the rescue on that morrow, so I bought two packets, just in case there's another drought in the near future.

Eventually, I managed to use up the stock and the resulting chicken and pea risotto was an unqualified success.

INGREDIENTS (serves two with loads of leftovers)

risotto rice 200gs
dash of dry white wine
chicken stock, about a pint
celery, one stalk finely chopped
onion, finely chopped
garlic, also finely chopped
big handful of frozen peas, thawed
chopped chicken, big handful
parmesan, another big handful, plus extra for sprinkling
butter, knob there of
olive oil, dash

THE PLAN

Start off by gently frying the onion and celery and garlic in the olive oil in a sauce pan with a pinch of salt without colouring until soft. This will probably take about 10 -15 minutes or so.

As that's happening, sort out the chicken stock and keep warm.

When the vegetables are soft, turn up the heat up to a medium setting and add the rice. Get ready for the stirring. Mix well and stir fry the rice for a minute or two until shiny. Now add the white wine and continue stirring. Keep stirring until the alcohol is all burned off (ie you can't smell it any more) and then add your first ladleful of stock. When you do this add another small pinch of salt and pepper and stir around some more.

Ideally, you want the rice at a lively simmer. So just keep adding the stock and massaging the rice, allowing each ladleful to be absorbed before you add the next one. This should take about 20 to 25 minutes after which time, the rice should be nicely tender but still with a very slight bite. If you happen to run out of stock, fear not, just add some hot water.

When the rice is tender, check the seasoning and remove from the heat. Add the butter and the parmesan and the thawed peas and the chicken and stir it all up. This is the important bit: Put a lid on the pot and leave it to stand for two full minutes. If you're like me, the anticipation should be killing you at this stage but by leaving the risotto sit, it will develop a delicious oozing texture.

Ladle into bowls, add another touch of parmesan and a few thyme leaves and devour without delay.

If you've had to trek all over the country to track down the rice, the resulting risotto will taste all the better. And if you've made the chicken stock yourself – and it didn't go to waste – you'll be all the happier.

---

when you're not quite sweet enough
sweet strawberry risotto

IF I have learned anything about myself thus far, I have to admit, I'm not much of a dessert man – apart from ice-cream which is the chilly exception to the rule. Real vanilla ice-cream is a joyous thing and more often than not I keep a constant supply in the freezer. It does wonders for one's morale when the going gets tough – most Monday evenings, to be fair.

And yet, there are a another few 'sweets' I consider worth the effort, strawberry cheese cake is one that springs to mind – oh – and crème brûlée. It's not that I don't like sweet things, but rather if I've gone to the trouble of making dinner, I'll often find that I can't summon up the energy to make dessert – hence the ice-cream in the fridge.

Sweet strawberry risotto is another exception to the rule, though I could count on one hand the number of times I've summoned up the energy in the past 12 months. And yet, every single time I make it, I always tell myself I'll have to make it more often. It's seriously good.

Basically, if you can make ordinary risotto you can make sweet. It's like rice pudding only better and I think it works great as a late supper on a rainy Monday night.

INGREDIENTS (serves 4)

big handful of ripe strawberries
2 tablespoons of caster sugar
dash of orange juice
dash of water
dash of white wine
1 vanilla pod
big knob of butter
160g of risotto rice
pint of milk – full fat of course
dash of white wine
4 squares of dark chocolate
50g of white chocolate

THE PLAN

Start off by preparing the strawberries. Wash and hull and slice and then place in a small pan with one tablespoon of sugar and those dashes of orange juice and water. Turn up the heat and cook, stirring for a minute or two, until the sugar is dissolved and the strawberry juices are running. You don't want to cook it so much that the strawberries turn to mush, just so they're tender. Also, it should smell divine.

Now, in a thick-bottomed sauce pan, melt the butter and while that's happening, cut the vanilla pod in half and extricate the seeds by running the back of a knife down its inside. Add these tiny taste bombs to the butter and stir around. Dump in the rice and the second tablespoon of sugar, turn up the heat and stir fry for another 30 seconds. Add the wine and continue stirring and massaging until all the alcohol has burned away.

Now all you have to do is gradually add the milk, just like you would normally do with the stock. Keep going until the pint is incorporated, this should take around 15 minutes at a moderate simmer. Taste the rice and when it's tender it's ready. You can always add another jag of milk if needs be or another touch of sugar if you think it isn't sweet enough.

At this stage with normal risotto you would add the parmesan and allow to rest. So instead of the cheese, add the grated white chocolate, stir it in, bag a lid on and allow the risotto to sit for at least 60 seconds.

Ladle out into bowls, press a single square of dark choc into the middle of each bowl – it should disappear nicely – and then spoon some of the strawberry sauce over the top and tuck in without delay.

This is the perfect dessert for people who don't like desserts. Creamy, bright and moreish, it never fails to put a smile on my face.

g-knock up some gnocchi
simple gnocchi

SOMEONE far wiser than me once said that baked potatoes are a great vehicle for increasing a person's intake of butter – and I have to say, I heartily agree.

Irish people in general though, eat far too much butter, loaded as it is with saturated fats of dairy origin; although you could say the same thing about us in terms of alcohol and potatoes and chocolate. The Japanese diet is apparently the healthiest in the world, given their predilection to fruits of the sea but even they have their culinary vices - - whale and dolphin meat isn't exactly PC.

> It isn't fancy and it isn't complicatied but in terms of taste, it's simple and virtually unbeatable and, as I mentioned, a great vehicle for increasing one's intake of butter.

Butter, as I always say is most often consumed in my house in and around recipes and the olive oil based spreads are the mainstay of toast and bread and the like. The best substitute spreads are just that, substitutes although some are perfectly acceptable in a second class, I'm-watching-my-cholestrol kind of way.

However sometimes, nothing else is going to do except butter and I feel, when it is necessary, you have to make that conscious choice and relish your decision. Take delight in the treat with the knowledge that it is only a treat and you'll enjoy it all the more.

I have devoured gnocchi is various ways over the years in tomato sauce, smothered in Cashel Blue, in cream with walnuts and melted Gruyere or on their own with plenty of seasoning and a dusting of parmesan. Whatever their mode of consumption the cheese has been ever present and I eat the little dumplings slowly and deliberately, savouring every mouthful of simplicity with a glass of deep redness. They can be wonderfully satisfying or, when under-seasoned, wonderfully bland but thankfully the former is no great mission to achieve.

My favourite way to scoff gnocchi, as you may have guessed, is to treat them (and myself) with a dose of butter and some sprinklings of cheese. It isn't fancy and it isn't complicated but in terms of taste, it's simple and virtually unbeatable and, as I mentioned, a great vehicle for increasing one's intake of butter.

Basically potato bread in the form of dumplings, these little bombs are deceptively easy to make. You could buy them pre-packed but they'll have nowhere near the same taste or texture.

INGREDIENTS

500g or thereabouts of potatoes
200g of plain flour
plenty of seasoning
at least a tablespoon of butter
a good handful of grated parmesan

This is almost as easy as boiling a pot of spuds.

Start off by doing just that, boil or steam your spuds until tender and then allow to steam dry a little and mash thoroughly WITHOUT butter or milk. Season generously and taste to make sure the mash isn't bland.

Add the flour and mix until you have a ball of dough. Then, on a lightly floured surface, roll out a sausage of dough and cut into small sections. I like my gnocchi bigger than bite size, so something slightly smaller than the size of a golf ball is perfect. Roll the cuts into the small balls and then press each ball with a fork and remove to a large floured baking tray.

Set a large saucepan of salted water to simmering and then cook off your gnocchi in batches, a few at a time.

You'll know when each individual gnocchi is cooked through because it will float to the top. Repeat until they are all cooked and then place in bowls, cover with the cheese and dot with the butter and blast under a hot grill for a minute or until the cheese is melted and you can't wait any longer. Serve with yet more cheese and if they need it, another grinding of black pepper and a touch of sea salt.

Sometimes, the simple things really are the best.

six... bedtime stories

elvis

IT was with some concern that I recently read headlines about Scottish GPs voting on a proposal to have chocolate taxed in the same way as alcohol and cigarettes. Not that I'm that much of a fan of choc mind you, but isn't our nanny state bureaucratised enough?

It was therefore with some relief that I learned that the chocolate tax was subsequently defeated by two votes – a close call.

Things are becoming desperate in Scotland, it is true; the country has the second highest level of obesity in the developed world (after America) but surely this is no reason to abandon common sense. Why punish the majority for the weaknesses of the minority?

I recall the government was also talking about having a minimum price for alcohol because apparently people are drinking too much. This is news to me; I can personally affirm, I'm not drinking half enough.

Similarly, last year the House of Lords had a debate on restricting the sale of thick-sliced bread so that our packed lunches are less fattening. Unbelievable, but good work if you can get it.

It's funny (funny strange, not funny haha) how the machinations of government work. When you'd imagine they should all be sitting around working out how we're going to defeat global warming or the credit crunch, in reality it would appear that ministers and government officials are all staggering around the House of Commons (or Stormont) with blank looks on their faces, bumping into one another.

"What will we have a debate on today?"

"What about the thickness of sliced bread? Oooorrrrr, what about foods beginning with 'B'?"

Nice work if you can get it.

At times like these I am reminded of Elvis, now there was a man who wasn't afraid to eat thick slices of bread. OK, so he kicked his Tennessee bucket in extreme and infamous circumstances, but I'd bet my bottom dollar he was a fun man to be around.

Once upon a time, on the night of February 1 1976 to be exact, the day I was born, funnily enough, Elvis was at his home, Graceland in Memphis.

The great man was hanging out with some buddies including Jerry Kennedy of the Colorado Police Force and Ron Pietrafeso from a specialist anti-crime strike force.

Conversation, as is often the case, turned to food and specifically the infamous Fool's Gold Loaf which the Colorado Mine Company restaurant in Denver was fond of serving. The loaf, which took its name from its hefty price tag ($49.95) consisted of an entire loaf filled with a whole host of fattening culinary paraphernalia.

One loaf of Italian bread is coated with a handful of softened butter. This is roasted in an oven for 15 or so minutes until golden. The bread is split down the middle, the soft inside is scrapped out to allow room for the filling and then is filled thus: One whole jar of peanut butter, one jar of grape jelly, and a pound of bacon, fried crispy and still warm.

Elvis, as was his wont, had to have one there and then.

The three lads (plus whoever else was hanging around and happened to be hungry), went out the back of Graceland, jumped into Elvis's private jet, the Lisa Marie, and flew nearly 1,000 miles, two hours to Denver in search of some Fools Gold.

Upon arrival, the Lisa Marie taxied to a special hangar where the passengers were greeted by the owner of the Colorado Mine Company, Buck Scott, and his wife Cindy who had brought 22 fresh Fool's Gold Loaves for the men. Elvis and co washed the sarnies down with Perrier and champagne and when they were finished, flew back to Graceland without ever having left the airport. Now that's what I call rock and roll.

I wonder if Elvis was of Scottish descent.

I recall the government was also talking about having a minimum price for alcohol because apparently people are drinking too much. This is news to me; I can personally affirm, I'm not drinking half enough.

it's a sin to kill a mockingbird

FRANCE 1995... Controversial French president (and alleged Nazi collaborator) Francois Mitterand is nearing the end of his reign in office. Diagnosed earlier with prostate cancer, as December arrives, France's first socialist leader knows the reek of The Grim Reaper's breath. He decides, as many of us might, to have one last hurrah and invites a load of his friends around for a final feast.

The menu, chosen by the host himself, is the best of traditional French cuisine. To start, diners are presented with the finest foie gras and oysters. Then comes the centre piece of the meal, the ortolan.

A tiny and very rare songbird, the ortolan is a member of the bunting family and is a protected species in Europe. It is so rare, in fact, that eating the ortolan is against French law.

The birds are caught in the wild, blinded and fed to four times their natural size. Then, before Mitterand's feast, their tiny lives are extinguished by drowning in hot Armagnac. A brief time in the oven and soon they're on the plate.

Mitterand's assembled diners then cover their heads with a shroud-like cloth, this serves two purposes. First, none of the aroma from the tiny meal will escape and also, the act will be hidden from God.

"Devotees claim they can taste the bird's entire life as they chew in the darkness: the wheat of Morocco, the salt air of the Mediterranean, the lavender of Provence. The pea-sized lungs and heart, saturated with Armagnac from its drowning, are said to burst in a liqueur-scented flower on the diner's tongue." – In the Devil's Garden - A Sinful History of Forbidden Food.

Eaten whole, bones and all, fanatics say that devouring the ortolan is like tasting the soul of France itself.

In a recent programme for BBC FOUR entitled France on a Plate, Cultural historian Andrew Hussey investigated the reasons for this illicit banquet. Why had food become so important to the French that they would turn a blind eye to their democratically elected leader eating an endangered species?

What happened to Monsieur Mitterand? Well, the gluttonous, law-flouting emperor scoffed not one but two of the rare birds.

They were the last food he ever ate.

Apart from wondering about the state of France in modern Europe, hearing about Mitterand's final meal has made me think. Would I eat an ortolan? But more importantly, what would I like for my final meal?

The curious glutton in me can't help but wonder what the soul of France tastes like, but I reckon, all things considered, I'd pass on the rare songbird. Any food you have to hide from God can't be a good thing. And what is more, I think there's just something inherently wrong about eating a songbird. It puts me in mind of Harpur Lee's To Kill a Mockingbird.

When Jem and Scout receive a gun each as a present, Atticus advises them, "I'd rather you shot at tin cans in the back yard, but I know you'll go after birds. Shoot all the bluejays you want, if you can hit 'em, but remember it's a sin to kill a mockingbird."

And I'm afraid my last hurrah in culinary terms would be a much more mundane affair than Mitterand's.

A brace of softly poached duck eggs on toasted white bread with oodles of real butter, a dusting of salt and some freshly ground black pepper. Then a double espresso and a Kitkat.

Haute cuisine or what!

---

another leetle french man

MANY moons ago, I left college, shouldered a rucksack and travelled to Dublin to make my fortune – it was all very exciting. Not really having much of a clue what I was at, I somehow managed to blag my way into a job as a computer/internet support person and was mightily chuffed with myself at the prospect. It was my first job and also, I could barely switch a computer on.

New work meant new money and a new and exciting phenomenon for me at this time was disposable income; as little as I was making, I felt like a millionaire. I rented an apartment, bought a cork screw, some Paris buns and a video recorder and set about living the high life. A quare bon viveur, I considered myself to be, eating out three nights a week and maybe again at the weekends. I think I was even considering investing in a monocle and a brass tipped walking stick.

Anyway... I remember one night out, myself and the missus were propping up a bar on the latest fashionable eatery on the South-side waiting for a table to become available when we noticed a Frenchman send his plate back.

We could tell he was French by the cut of his jib (plus I wasn't long back from a year 'en France') but we couldn't hear what was being said except that he was smiling when the waitress took the plate away.

Moments later we were seated at an adjacent table, inadvertently and unintentionally eavesdropping on the Gallic conversation. Everything was incroyable (unbelievable) and pénible (tiresome).

Perusing the menu with a grin, I recall being caught between carpaccio and pizza (it's funny the details the brain retains). Several minutes later the waitress returned but again, the Frenchman sent her packing, this time with a few words of advice.

"I want ze steak bleu. You understand me? BLEU!" And to give the waitress a tip to pass on to the chef, held out his hands, touched one palm to the other, made a frying sound, then flipped the top hand on it's back and made another frying sound.

As far as I am aware ze leetle French man got his wish because the next time his steak arrived he wasted no time before tucking in, releasing a few moans for good measure/pleasure.

And guess what I had to have when the harassed waitress finally arrived to take our order. You betcha. It had to be a blue steak – only this time without the hand mimes.

I can't remember if the resulting blue was any good or not – that's exactly how good it was. It was a fillet, that much I do recall.

Sometimes something of a let-down, over-cooked or under-cooked or just simply bland, when a really good steak arrives, it's always enough to know your socks off. Personal preference goes a long way though I am partial to a sirloin from time to time – medium to rare. That said, I could count on one hand the number of times I've ordered steak when I've been out for a meal. It's not that the great restaurants of this world don't do a great steak, it's just that great steak is perfectly achievable at home and at a fraction of the price.

---

super soup

THERE'S just something so fulfilling about slurping soup (and slittering it all down your shirt) when it's cold and raining outside. I don't know why, but wind whistling down the chimney and the letterbox rattling somehow makes it taste better.

For meteorological reasons (mainly) Irish people in general don't really go in for cold soups – gazpacho and the like – even at the height of summer when the letterbox is rattling and the hail is pumping down the chimney and into the living-room. Though hot and savoury stuff aside, there is a whole world of soups out there that most people aren't even aware exists. We all know of the scotch broths, cock-a-leekies, minestrones and bouillabaisses but have you ever heard of fanesca (a traditional cod soup from Ecuador) or tarator (a Bulgarian cold soup made from yoghurt and cucumbers)? Or my personal favourite (I haven't tried it but it sounds so bizarre it has to be class) ginataan, a Filipino soup made from coconut milk, milk, fruits and tapioca pearls, served cold.

Sometimes we think we invent everything, but chances are, if you can think of another culture, then they have their favourite soup too.

Something that we are not overly familiar with in this part of the world are fruit soups. Served hot or cold depending on the recipe, many recipes are for cold soups served when fruit was in season during hot weather. Some like Norwegian fruktsupp may be served hot and rely on dried fruit such as raisins and prunes and so could be made in any season. Fruit soups may also include milk, sweet or savoury dumplings, spices, or alcoholic beverages like brandy or champagne. Chilly (as in cold) fruit soups are most common in Scandinavian, Baltic and Eastern European cuisines, while hot fruit soups with meat appear in Middle Eastern, Central Asian and Chinese cuisines.

Historically, the term soup originates from the Teutonic word suppa, which refers to a Medieval dish comprising a thick stew poured on top of slices of bread, called sop, used to soak up the liquid. Often described as potages, French onion soup is an example of a modern soup that retains this bread sop.

And get this: The word restaurant was first used in France in the 16th century to describe a highly concentrated, inexpensive soup, sold by street vendors called restaurer, that was advertised as an antidote to physical exhaustion. In 1765, a Parisian entrepreneur opened a shop specialising in restaurers. This prompted the use of the modern word restaurant to describe the shops. All thanks to the humble soup!

Portable soup was devised in the 18th century by boiling seasoned meat until a thick, resinous syrup was left that could be dried and stored for months at a time. The Japanese miso is an example of a concentrated soup paste.

We all have our favourite soups of course (and if you're reading this in Tyrone then chances are, potato and leek is up there with yours) but have you ever wondered what the choice of the stars is? You can tell a lot by a person's favourite soup, I reckon.

Tony Blair's favourite is apparently Carrot and Sweet Potato; Hitler's mistress, Eva Braun's was Turtle Soup; Charles Darwin's was Young Tortoise Soup (no wonder he was always hanging around the Galapogos); Frederick the Great's favourite was Beer Soup but Braveheart himself has to take away the 'Strange' award. Mel Gibson's best soup is Chinese Mystery Soup.

Mel explains, "The next morning [in Taipei], I had a headache you couldn't believe, so he took me to this marketplace and got me a bowl of soup. It was a slightly murky broth with what looked like the endocrine glands and digestive tract of a small animal, the intact oesophagus, liver, lungs, pancreas, intestines and adrenal glands. I never knew what it was, but it was delicious. I ate it all and felt great afterward. They know something, the Chinese." (from a Playboy interview, 1995).

Don't be going and thinking I read Playboy though. I only look at the pictures.

And get this: The word restaurant was first used in France in the 16th century to describe a highly concentrated, inexpensive soup, sold by street vendors called restaurer, that was advertised as an antidote to physical exhaustion.

I KNOW a pleasant chap who reckons "Everything always comes back to kung-fu." I'm not entirely sure what this means but if I think about it and try to translate things onto a personal basis, in my case, everything always comes back to food.

This cropped up in the work tea room once when someone mentioned the French town of Toulouse. Someone else pointed out that it was an unfortunate name for any sporting teams which might be playing their wares in the locality and quasi-subconsciously I added, "Good sausages though."

I'm not sure if there is a special connection between my stomach and my brain or if I'm just predisposed to thinking about my next meal, but whatever the case you can simplify things by saying, "everything comes back to food."

I was watching as bit of the Masters golf from Augusta that same week, when Tiger Woods happened to be playing. The good wife reckoned that given his recent sowing of genetically modified oats, this is all he will be remembered for – despite being one of the best golfers ever to have picked up a club.

Now, I'm not sure if I agree with this sentiment or not but... say for example I was to find out that Tiger's favourite food is (for argument sake) pavlova. Every time I'd see him again the image of a pavlova would spring unbidden into my head. Everything comes back to food.

And so it will be with Lee Marvin.

My father told me a story recently about the Academy Award-winning actor and regardless of whatever film he has ever been in (Dirty Dozen etc) or whatever else he achieved in his life (he fought in World War II and was subsequently awarded the Purple Heart), Mr Marvin will henceforward be remembered for one thing and one thing only.

Apparently, Lee was something of a hell-raiser in his younger days and liked nothing better than painting the town red. Asked once by a reporter if he was a genial drunk or a belligerent one?

Lee replied, "It depends on what I'm drinking, how much I'm drinking, why I'm drinking, and who I'm drinking with."

However in-between bouts of hitting the bottle (or strangers over the head with a banjo – this actually happened once in a bar in LA), Lee liked nothing better than complaining about his wife's food.

So often and publicly and loudly did Mr Marvin complain about Mrs Marvin's home-cooking, one night, Mrs Marvin decided enough was enough.True to form, Lee landed in from one of his frequent benders only to find that for dinner, his wife had cut out a cardboard picture of a roast dinner and had set it onto his plate.

Without missing a beat Lee proceeded to eat the entire cardboard cut-out and what is more, said it was the best meal she had ever cooked for him.

I can't for this life of me find out which wife this story relates to but he was married twice and had at least one long-term co-habitation partner.

It's just a good thing that in Lee's case, everything didn't come back to kung-fu.

EVERY Christmas it's always the same: I always tell myself I'm going to have to start eating more healthily, my trousers and Christmas belt always demand it.

No more beer for at least the month of January (discounting one's birthday of course) and once the butter's gone I'm back on to olive or sunflower oil spreads. Definitely no more Celebrations, Roses or Quality Street (I think I ate all the Purple Ones in the world anyway) and sugar in general is off the menu altogether.

Oats too, will be high on the agenda for 2010, the wonder food that they are. Not only are they clinically proven to help lower cholesterol and therefore reduce the risk of heart disease, they also make you feel fuller for longer which means that you eat less over the course of a day (if you have them for breakfast). They also help with blood pressure and contain anti-cancer properties and in short are pretty much the best stuff you can be putting into your cake hole on a regular basis.

But as the lad from the Bran Flakes ad used to say, "One step at a time, Martin."

Before oats take over my culinary world, I must mention one of my gastronomic revelations from the festive period. Truffles.

Part of my brother's much-too-generous Christmas pressie this year was a little jar of truffle slices. Italian and languishing beneath a layer of olive oil, the truffle discs looked dangerously tasty.

Anyway, returning home clutching my little jar I couldn't wait to try them out and at approximately 2am on Boxing Day morning, I sat down to the best scrambled eggs of 2009 – and possibly the best scrambled eggs I have ever eaten.

There's no real way of describing the truffle taste, except to say it's unlike anything you have ever tasted and is something of an acquired flavour. The truffle tang is unfathomably deep and thick and earthy, something you might imagine yourself eating at a wizard's log cabin in the woods after becoming lost at dusk. Faintly magical and very moreish, it's all the more delectable because – for me at least – it's a once in a blue moon sensation.

Not to be confused with the chocolate treat of the same name, truffles are a fungi often referred to as 'diamond of the kitchen'. The finest truffle is reputed to be the most expensive foodstuff in the world, though I am at a loss as to whether they are to be found in Tyrone and Ireland. I suppose if you are finding truffles on a regular basis with the help of hound or swine, this is a tasty morsel of information you would likely keep to yourself.

On in the early hours of Boxing Morning, I reluctantly restricted myself to about a quarter of the jar and a teaspoon of the oil, doused across the eggs with a grinding of pepper and a touch of salt for good measure. I went to bed a happy man that night and repeated the experience for breakfast a day later.

I wonder now that the jar is gone if I should invest in another. I wonder also if I should investigate whether wild truffles are available locally. And I wonder if they are, should I procure a dog or a pig to help me locate said fungi. Pigs, I understand have an innate ability to scent out the truffle in the wood, though dogs can be trained. Dogs would be easier to control should they find a treasure, whereas the pig would want to scoff the truffle on sight.

This, I can relate to.

There's no real way of describing the truffle taste, except to say it's unlike anything you have ever tasted and is something of an acquired flavour. The truffle tang is unfathomably deep and thick and earthy, something you might imagine yourself eating at a wizard's log cabin in the woods after becoming lost at dusk.

seven... cheers

warm your heart
mulled wine

UP until the first time I made some for myself (that is to say, home-made), I had very little time for the mulled drinks of this world.

Hot whiskeys apart, wine and certainly cider were not, as far as I could comprehend, supposed to be hot. If you wanted warming through after an afternoon outside in the bleak mid-winter, then you could have a cup of hot tea, soup or even hot chocolate. Wine? No chance. Cider? Get thee behind me, Satan.

How wrong was I?

There is nothing – and I mean nothing – like a mug of steaming mulled wine for bringing a flush to your cheeks and a warm, cosy feeling to your belly.

It probably wouldn't work in quite the same way in summer but during winter, with the wind blowing everyone's heads away and the rain doing its level best to wash our faces off, mulled wine on a chilly and blustery Saturday evening is unbeatable. But don't just take my word for it.

Even if you're not a wine drinker, you are guaranteed to love a mug of the warm, sweetened stuff. Arguably the best thing about it (apart from the taste, feeling, aroma and sensation) is that since you're going to radically alter the taste of the wine – through the mulling procedure – then you don't have to shell out an appendage for a vintage bottle, any cheap stuff will do.

There are probably several ways to mull a wine but this way is one of the easiest and most effective.

INGREDIENTS

1 bottle of cheap red plonk
2 cinnamon sticks (broken)
5 cloves
pinch of nutmeg (ideally freshly grated)
cup of water (the amount doesn't have to be too precise)
2 heaped tablespoons of demerara sugar
2 heaped tablespoons of honey
1 orange, halved and juiced

THE PLAN

It couldn't be simpler – bang all your ingredients into a big pot, stir it all up and heat through but don't boil. Once it's heated, taste for sweetness and add more sugar if necessary.

Once you've tried this and get the knack (there's very little to it, in all honesty) you can add other things to spice it up. A shot of brandy or whisky, some slices of lemon, chopped grapes, apples, pomegranate, cranberry juice – there's no accounting for taste.

Mulled wine works well, both as an aperitif and an after dinner sweetener, but for maximum decadence (something often forgotten about around Christmas time) drink a mug with a left over mince pie or some crumbly apple tart. Heavenly doesn't even begin to describe it.   The effects of the wine are predictable enough but combined with the mild euphoria from the nutmeg, the sedative effects of the honey, the seductive dark sugar and the freshness of the orange (or other fruit), the whole shebang creates a wondrously comforting and relaxing marvel. It's like liquid comfort food, only tastier and it assaults all the senses. If mulled wine could sing it would take over the world.

There is nothing – and I mean nothing – like a mug of steaming mulled wine for bringing a flush to your cheeks and a warm, cosy feeling to your belly.

cocktails...
and a long island iced tea

THERE's just something about warm, balmy weather that puts you in the form for drinking – and I'm not talking about quenching thirst or any of that malarkey – although there's a lot to be said for that too. I'm referring to drinking: Getting tanked; laying siege to the bar; praising the great god of the ancients, Al Hugh Hol; a night on the tiles; heading out on a session or even sipping something cool in your own personal (beer) garden. Drinking.

Although practically unbeatable on a warm day, a cold beer can be ordered at any time of the year, but with the onset of spring and summer, what could be better than an ice-cold cocktail, lovingly prepared to your own personal taste. Apart from the hangover (well documented and experienced by people all over the world), the other downside to cocktails is that they tend to taste so good, you soon find yourself staggering about, slurring your speech and haranguing complete strangers. "Did anybody – hic – ever tell you thomthing? Know, you're lethal!" This is especially dangerous on the Friday night after payday, when, if you're not careful, you can tend to think you're JR.

"Put that money away – I'm buying the drinkth – hic!"

There are many and varied theories as to the origin of the word 'cocktail' but since they're all long-winded and dusty, we'll forget about them for the purpose of time and space.

Just like the little girl with the curl, when they (cocktails) are good the are very, very good, but when they are bad, they are horrid.

Rising to popularity during the prohibition era in the United States, primarily to mask the taste of bootlegged alcohol, cocktails were mixed by bartenders at speakeasies, incorporating many ingredients, both alcoholic and non (every cloud and all that). However, one of the oldest known cocktails, the Cognac-based Sazerac, dates from 1850s New Orleans, as many as 70 years prior to the Prohibition era.

Everyone has their own particular sensibilities when it comes to cocktails and thankfully, there is no end of combinations vying for your tasting custom.

As a greenhorned student, my preferred cocktail of choice was the Snakebite (1/2 pint of beer and 1/2 pint of cider) although these could be quite sickening if you morphed into a stetson-wearing Texan. As I remember, a jag of blackcurrent diluting juice was required to make it halfway drinkable. For the initiated, adding a shot of Pernod to this turning it into a Purple Diesel. Then adding three shots of vodka to a Purple Diesel made a 'Screaming Purple Bastard' - although this is worryingly descriptive of the result of drinking one.

The Wild Boar was another cocktail I once encountered during a brief sojourn in Corsica and

> Just like the little girl with the curl, when they (cocktails) are good the are very, very good, but when they are bad, they are horrid.

after three of these, the evening went by in a flash.

THE (WAYWARD) PLAN

Take one pint glass and fill to two inches off the top with beer. Pour in one inch of whisky (ideally manufactured by a slack-jawed crone in a still behind the bar). Turn your back to the bar and throw a coin over your shoulder. Then fill the glass to the top with whatever bottle you hit.

After you down two, this cocktail is also know as the 'What Are You Thayin' Now?'

But for maximum effect, when you want to go from vertical to horizontal with the minimum amount of fuss, there is no better man than Knockout Juice.

THE COMPONENTS

1 shot Jack Daniels
1 shot Southern Comfort
1 shot Tequila
1 shot whiskey
Lemonade to taste.

This should make half a pint and is also known as The Assassin – for obvious reasons – and the taste is best described as 'acquired'.

Alternatively, for the best of every dimension, there are few cocktails to match the salacious Long Island Iced Tea. On a lugubrious Sunday afternoon, one of these badboys is like an intravenous shot of heaven. Not only does it taste like the second batch of stuff they served at Cana, it also makes you feel like you've been visited by the Man Himself.

INGREDIENTS

1 measure vodka
1 measure triple sec
1 measure white rum
1 measure dark rum
1 measure tequila
Lemon and lime mixer, like 7up
A dash of Coke
Ice

METHOD

Mix the spirits with lots of ice then top up the glass with the lemon and lime mixer and add a dash of coke for colour/taste. Sen. Sa. Tional.

nearly as good as beer
sangria

WHAT'S the tastiest drink in existence when the world is drenched in sunshine and everyone's sweating like Christie Moore playing guitar in hell? Sorry, let me rephrase that question: What's the tastiest drink in the world *after beer*, when the world is drenched in sunshine and everyone's sweating like Christie Moore etc etc?

The answer can only be sangria.

I was forced into making sangria once when a friend came to visit and the world happened to be drenched in sunshine. I'd never done it before, but in the end, I was glad I did. I have since learned that you do not need to visit Spain (or even be an expert) to make great sangria. Ice-cold, infinitely fruity and deceptively drinkable, Michael's Home-made Sangria was a categorical success. The good news is, it's fool-proof and the best news is, it really hits the spot.

Traditionally a wine punch from Spain or Portugal, the word sangria comes from the Spanish sangre meaning 'blood' ('sangue' in Portuguese) and is usually made from red wine. Incidentally, if you used white, it would be called sangria blanca but whatever the alcohol base, the process couldn't be simpler.

Another thing I have learned is that sangria made a day in advance tastes a shade better. There are loads and loads of recipes for sangria on the doublya dou-blya doublya, but any variations on this following theme will work perfectly. This is actually a combination of two of the recipes. Any fruits could conceivably be used and I am told a peach really makes it, but these little hairy bums seem to be out of season whenever I'm making.

INGREDIENTS

1 bottle of fruity red wine (I used a cheap bottle of Spanish table wine)
the same quantity of the best apple/orange juice you can get your hands on
1 apple, chopped
1 pear, chopped
half a lemon, sliced
half an orange, sliced
1 heaped table spoon of honey
dash of brandy

THE PLAN

Combine your apple juice and red wine in a large jug and add all your sliced and chopped fruit – reserving a few nice slices for serving – along with the brand and sugar or honey. Stir is all up and mix, to allow the sugar to dissolve and then bang this jug into the fridge and allow to 'mature' for at least an hour.
After this time, pour out a tall glass of the sangria, top with a few ice-cubes and a slice or two or lemon and orange and drink without delay.

"IT is so long since I first took opium, that if it had been a trifling incident in my life, I might have forgotten its date: but cardinal events are not to be forgotten; and, from circumstances connected with it, I remember that it must be referred to the autumn of 1804."

In his book, Confessions of an English opium-eater, Thomas De Quincey outlines the gravity of having tasted opium for the first time. It was such a stupendously momentous occasion, he had been unable to eradicate the experience from his mind. I can relate to this – not the opiate – but the memory of the cardinal event.

It is so long since I had my first mojito, that if it had been a trifling incident in my life, I might have forgotten its date: but cardinal events are not to be forgotten.

I remember it well. I was living in Dublin at the time and on a balmy Saturday afternoon in Temple Bar, I was, for the umpteenth time, reading down through the list of cocktails unsure what to have. Something of a cocktailed greenhorn, I foolishly imagined all mixed drinks were overly sweet and eventually sickening and had been attempting to avoid the hangover in a glass.

"I might just stick to the beer," I recall offering, lamely.

"Come on, we all have to have one."

It was thus I relented (I have always been a sucker for peer pressure) and with the arrival of an unknown highball known as a mojito, my life was changed forever.

I have since learned that Ernest Hemingway was an ardent fan of the mojito and, if it's good enough for a Nobel Laureate, it's good enough for me. There's something deeply attractive about swilling back mojitos on a veranda somewhere in Cuba. Maybe that's where he came up with the story for The Old Man and the Sea.

Anyway... during the long evenings especially, sometimes we are in need of a little sunshine from time to time and barring a brief sojourn in Cuba, there are few drinks better at injecting a few joyous rays than a well-balanced mojito. Sweet and sour, refreshing and infinitely drinkable, a mojito often tastes too good.

This is so simple and there are so few elements, it hardly even qualifies as a recipe at all but can't recommend these highly enough.

INGREDIENTS (for one, though you'll no doubt come back for another)

two teaspoons of caster sugar
the juice of one lime (about two tablespoonfuls)
a quarter of a lime
4 mint leaves
sprig of mint
2 measures of white rum
fizzy water

THE PLAN

It couldn't be easier. In a wide glass, add the sugar, the lime juice, the lime quarter and the four mint leaves. Now gently mash the mixture with a fork or the back of a spoon (ideally you'd want a wooden device called a muddler but I don't have one) to crush the mint and lime and get the flavours going. Then add the crushed ice, the rum and a good dash of fizzy water. Stir, add another sprig of mint and taste. Add another dash of water if necessary and you're done.

Now all you need is the Buena Vista Social Club, some nachos and a little socialism and it's party time.

...Cardinal events are not to be forgotten.

sometimes we are in need of a little sunshine from time to time and barring a brief sojourn in Cuba, there are few drinks better at injecting a few joyous rays than a well-balanced mojito

"Si Dieu me prête vie, je ferai qu'il n'y aura point de laboureur en mon royaume qui n'ait les moyens d'avoir le dimanche une poule dans son pot!" Roughly translated, this means, "Lordo, cheer up lads, we're having chicken on Sunday!"

eight... cuisine most foul

feeding without effort
poule au pot (one pot chicken)

IN these times of economic decrepitude it's comforting to know that even the cheapest of Sunday banquets can be a sensational experience for the tastebuds.

Take poule au pot for example, now there's a cheap meal that just keeps on giving. Simplicity itself to prepare, this is a one pot dish which will not only provide you with a soup for starters, but also a wonderfully rustic meal, moist meat and a selection of roasted vegetables. This is no exaggeration: But by the time it takes your oven to pre-heat, you can have all the necessary work done to feed six people.

Legend has it that one time French king, Henri IV concerned about the well-being of his more financially challenged subjects, decided that a new dish must be created.

"Si Dieu me prête vie, je ferai qu'il n'y aura point de laboureur en mon royaume qui n'ait les moyens d'avoir le dimanche une poule dans son pot!"

Roughly translated, this means, "Lordo, cheer up lads, we're having chicken on Sunday!"

And lo it came to pass that poule au pot was born – all at the behest of a benevolent Huguenot king.

There are likely many and varied ways of fashioning poule au pot but the only things you really need is the poule and the pot – preferably with a lid. I use a big enamel dish my mother-in-law gave me as a present and it works a treat.

None of these vegetable ingredients are cast in stone, but the following seem to be regulars in my local supermarket all year round and as well, they will make an excellent soup.

INGREDIENTS

1 medium sized chicken
2 leeks
2 onions
four cloves of garlic
4 pommes de terre (spuds to you an' me)
2 parsnips
2 carrots
knob of butter
half a teaspoon of dried thyme
two bay leaves
big pinch of salt
black pepper
glass and a half of water

glug of dry white wine

Set your oven to pre-heating (190°C) and while that's happening, peel the spuds and wash and roughly chop the veg. This is peasant food and depending on the size of the chicken, will get about an hour and a half in the oven, so even the biggest spud will be cooked through.

Place the poule in the pot, strew the vegetables around the outside, pour over the wine and water, rub the butter and thyme into the breast and then season liberally with salt and freshly ground black pepper.

Stick the lid on and retire to the oven for one hour. After this time, remove the lid and baste the chicken. Give the veg a stir around as well and the return to the oven without the lid for another 35 minutes or so or until cooked through (the juices run clear).

Carve the chicken and serve in warmed bowls with a few of the vegetables drizzled with some of the buttery juices – oh– and some crusty bread for mopping.

If you were so inclined you could even keep the carcase and make some excellent stock...

"Si Dieu me prête vie..."

festive fare
stir fry cheesy turkey

I BET next New Year's Eve, you'll be wondering what all the fuss was about; the presents will all have been wrapped and opened and if you're like me, you'll be a few pounds heavier and paradoxically, quite a few pounds lighter.

We normally all eat turkey at some point over the festive period and chances are you're normally sick of the sight of the dry, often over-cooked meat. If you don't cook your own turkey next time round, and let's face it, most of us go free-loading for Christmas Day, ask your host for a doggy bag to take home with you for boxing day. Not only will they be more than glad to get rid, you will soon be over the moon with this new recipe for turkey leftovers.

Festive Stir Fried Cheesy turkey is so splendid, it can't be good for you and since it has double cream and loads of cheese in it, it's not good for you really. But then again, New Year's resolutions and Lent are just around the corner, so there's plenty of scope for shedding any unwanted timber.

INGREDIENTS (for one)

A handful or two of left over turkey, chopped up into small chunks
4 slices of streaky bacon chopped
4 spring onions, chopped
1 clove of garlic, chopped
olive oil
100 ml or about a good big glug of double cream
as many frozen peas as you can hold in one hand – unless of course your hands are abnormally large or small.
as many pasta shapes as you fancy scoffing, the little bows (farfalle) work well
Handful of grated parmesan
chopped mint (optional)
squirt of lemon juice (also optional but recommended)

THE PLAN

Set your pasta going and then fry up your bacon of choice in the olive oil until it's just about crisped. The fling in your spring onions (but only the white bits) and garlic, turn the heat down and stirfry until they're softened. You don't want to colour them up. Give your peas a minute in the microwave and then add them to the pan along with the turkey. After about another minute, stir in the cream, half the parmesan and some salt and pepper. Let it simmer away for a minute or two until the sauce has thickened a little and then dump in your drained pasta and toss it all around.

Serve it up in a big bowl with the rest of the parmesan over the top, the chopped green bits from the spring onions, a little chopped mint and the lemon juice. Some home-made garlic bread would go down well too and with a glass of chilly white wine, you'll have to resist licking the bowl.

If you have some left over ham, just add a handful of chopped pieces when you add the turkey. Or, instead of having the cheesy stir fry with pasta, why not try it with chips or mashed potatoes or even rice.

If you had the time (or could be bothered) you could even use the turkey and pea mix as a pie filling – just add loads of turkey so that it isn't too runny. Come to think of it, this filling would also go well in some vol au vent cases if some visitors landed round unexpectedly. It would also make a super topping for toast.

If you were feeling fancy, replace the peas with some asparagus spears.

If you don't cook your own turkey next time round, and let's face it, most of us go free-loading for Christmas Day, ask your host for a doggy bag to take home with you for boxing day. Not only will they be more than glad to get rid, you will soon be over the moon with this new recipe for turkey leftovers.

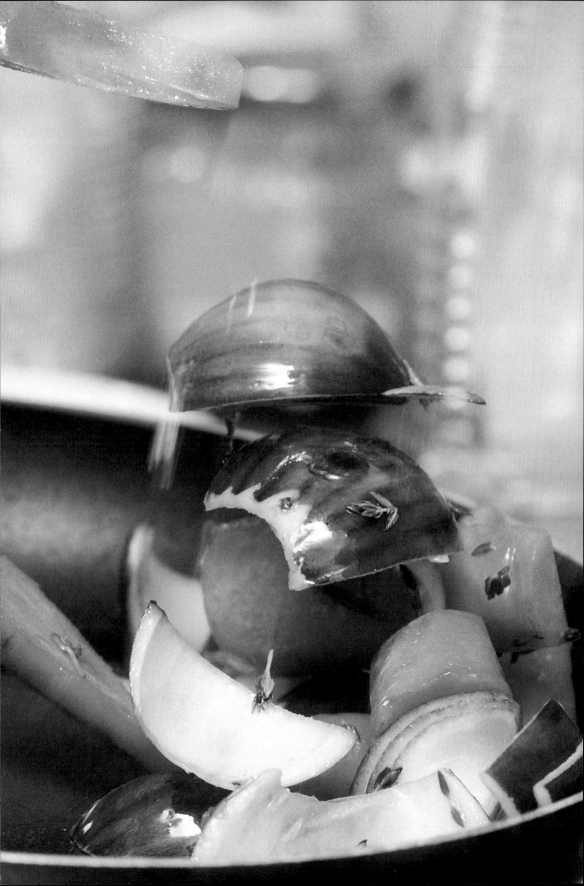

ruby murray
chicken tikka masala

APPARENTLY, if the statisticians are to be believed, one in seven curries sold in the UK and Ireland is a chicken tikka masala. This, I can well believe, as this creamy delight is often a mild dish where a lot of curry enthusiasts start.

Something of a bad rep because of insipid ready meals and the ubiquitous noodles, chicken tikka masala at a good restaurant or cooked at home with some diligence, can be a hugely rewarding – not to mention delicious – experience.

Preparing a curry from scratch isn't an enterprise to be entered into lightly; there's a marinating process and a whole range of spices but once you've tried it, you'll understand why it's worth the mission. This version of chicken tikka masala is an adaptation of a Jamie Oliver recipe – only I've tweaked it a little. The recipe is for two people and will leave you with enough sauce for chips the next night. If you're cooking for four, just double the chicken portions and you'll still have plenty of sauce.

INGREDIENTS

two chicken fillets, chopped into similar sized strips
150 ml of natural yoghurt
150 ml of double cream
dessertspoon of cashew butter
handful of chopped coriander
thumb-sized piece of ginger
5 big garlic cloves
two birdseye chillies, finely chopped
tbsp of paprika (not the smoked kind)
dessertspoon of cumin seeds, pounded
dessertspoon of coriander seeds, pounded
dessertspoon of chilli powder (you decide the heat factor)
two dessertspoons of garam masala
big pinch of mustard seeds
splash of sunflower oil
two dessert spoons of tomato purée or if you're stuck, tomato ketchup
two onions, finely sliced
big knob of butter
big pinch of sugar
half a pint of light chicken stock

THE PLAN

Finely grate the ginger and the garlic and dump in a bowl with the chopped chillies. Remember to discard the seeds if you don't want it too hot. Then with a good glug of sunflower oil in a frying pan, heat the mustard seeds until they start popping. Add these to the garlic and ginger mix along with the pounded cumin

and coriander seeds, one dessertspoon of the garam masala, the chilli powder and the paprika. Mix this all up and then divide between two bowls. Into one, add the chicken strips and the yoghurt, mix, cover with clingfilm and leave to chill out (in the fridge) over night or for a few hours at least.

The next day, or when it comes to dinner time, add the butter to a large frying pan and fry up the onions and the other half of the spice mix on a gentle heat for about 10 minutes. Add half a pint of water and half the pint of stock, the tomato purée, sugar and the cashew butter and simmer for a few minutes until the sauce reduces and thickens a bit. Check the seasoning and set aside.

At this stage your house should start to smell like an Indian restaurant, and if you're like me, you'll be pumping the popadums and the Cobra beer into you.

Take your marinating chicken out of the fridge and cook through under a hot grill. I normally place a layer of tinfoil onto the grill pan to save on the mess and subsequently a chewing from the missus. This process should only take about 7 or 8 minutes depending on the thickness of the chicken. Cut the biggest chunk in half to make sure they're done and try one for taste. They should be phenomenally good.

Re-heat the sauce and mix in the double cream and the second load of garam masala. As soon as it starts bubbling, take it off the heat and stir in the chicken. Taste for seasoning and that's it.

Serve with a squeeze of lime and sprinkle over the coriander. Also, I normally eat this with half rice and half nan bread and the last bottle of beer out of the four-pack.

It's a mission but it's unbelievably tasty.

stuffing and stuff

IT'S almost better than the Christmas day dinner itself... we're talking serious taste. Picture the scene: Several hours after you've first eaten a belly-load (but-guster) of turkey with all the trimmings, you wake up in front of Indiana Jones and the Temple of Doom, the green paper crown has slipped to the side and you're still surprised that you're wearing Homer Simpson bedroom slippers two sizes too big for you. Guts a-rumble you head for the kitchen. You couldn't manage any dessert the first time round and you're not going to start now. What's this? Is that a load of stuffing left?

Arguably the highlight of the festive fare, stuffing (properly done), oozes delection and comfort. Real, strong and herby, tangy stuffing, crunchy on top where it burst out of the bird but yet moist within, where all the juices have flowed in and amalgamated with the bread... oh, yeah!

For the life of me I cannot understand how people can go in for the dry alternative. You might as well grate a bit of toast and fling that around the plate. And as for that other stuff, the well-known brand (alternative) to real stuffing – you wouldn't (couldn't) give it to your dog – and he or she would sully their chops with it anyway.

Real stuffing, seasoned with the running fat is unbeatable for taste and yet it's so easy to make. Around this neck of the woods we normally limit ourselves to stuffing poultry but a whole variety of other stuff can be stuffed.

In addition to stuffing the body cavity of animals, including mammals, birds, and fish, various joints of larger animals may be stuffed after they have been deboned or a pouch has been cut into the joint. Popular recipes around the globe include stuffed chicken legs and stuffed breast of veal, as well as the traditional holiday stuffed goose or turkey. Many types of vegetables are also suitable for stuffing after their seeds or marrow has been removed. Tomatoes, capsicums (sweet or hot peppers) and vegetable marrows (zucchini) may be prepared in this way. Cabbages and similar vegetables can also be stuffed – outrageous! They are usually blanched first, in order to make their leaves more pliable – but that's another story. Historically even the romans enjoyed a bit of stuffing from time to time. The Roman cookbook 'De re coquinaria' by someone whose name escapes me, contains recipes for stuffed chicken, hare, pig, and even dormouse. In the Middle Ages, stuffing was known as farce, from the Latin farcire (via the French farcir), which means to stuff (get it in there!). The term stuffing first appears in English print circa 1538. After about 1880, the term stuffing was replaced by dressing in Victorian English. Today, both terms are used although the latter is more widely used on the far side of the pond.

It is occasionally claimed that the ancient Romans, as well as medieval cooks stuffed animals with other animals. An anonymous Andalusian cookbook from the 13th century includes a recipe for a ram stuffed with small birds. And, you won't get this one around any of the eateries in Beragh, there exists a similar recipe for a camel stuffed with sheep stuffed with bustards stuffed with carp stuffed with eggs, is mentioned in TC Boyle's book, 'Water Music'.

The stuff of wonder, stuffing is.

soup for the soul
chicken broth

I HAD the flu once and before you think it, no, it wasn't swine-flu. It was co-incidental, I'll grant you, that I was coming down with something just when the rest of the world was gearing itself up for a pandemic of the dreaded malady.

The thing is: When you're sick – with the flu or the cold or whatever – you're sense of humour goes out the window and text messages asking whether or not you'd "come out in a rasher" or have "applied your oinkment" weren't really appreciated. Of course, it's easy to be facetious about swine-flu although perhaps not entirely felicitous – especially when people are perishing – but losing our sense of humour is always a step in the wrong direction.

Anyway, since I was feeling poorly, I decided to fashion some chicken soup in a bid to rein in the self-pity (men make the worst patients, I admit).

A traditional remedy for colds and the like, chicken soup has been prescribed by doctors and quacks alike down through the centuries. Most recently, research conducted by Dr Stephen Rennard, professor of pulmonary and critical care medicine, and his colleagues at the University of Nebraska Medical Centre in Omaha, have studied the medicinal activity in chicken soup. They found that some components of the chicken soup inhibit neutrophil migration, which may have an anti-inflammatory effect that could hypothetically lead to temporary ease from symptoms of illness. In layman's terms, it makes you feel better.

However, there is no further clinical or scientific evidence that supports the medical properties of chicken soup – or so the internet tells me. And yet, if you're ever had the cold and have imbibed real, home-made chicken soup, it always seems to help a little – at least I think so anyway. Bearing this in mind, I dug out the stock pot and fired up the hob.

Making a chicken broth is simplicity itself, which is handy if you're light-headed and staggering around the kitchen coughing and sneezing and blowing your nose. Effectively all you're doing is boiling up a chicken so after you've added the contents to the pot, 1 hour and 20 minutes later, you're ready for your soup/treatment.

INGREDIENTS

1 normal sized chicken (I don't know what weight a normal sized chicken is but just make sure you've a pot big enough to hold chosen foul)
2 carrots
1 leek
1 stalk of celery
1 bay leaf
1 sprig of rosemary
1 sprig of thyme
big pinch of flatleaf parsley
water
seasoning

Wash and roughly chop the carrots and leeks and add to a large pot with the chicken, rosemary, thyme and the bay leaf. Cover with water, add a lid, bring to the boil and simmer gently for the aforementioned time. Check it every so often and skim any white scum from the surface of the broth.

After the allotted time, remove the cooked bird and strain the broth to remove any veg. Return the liquid to the hob, return to the boil and reduce by one third.

Now, when this is done, you should have a nearly clear chicken broth and to this you can add whatever you like: a few chopped spring onions, some chilli pepper slices, mushrooms, some shards of the chicken itself, cooked rice – the list is long if it's imaginative.

I however, knocked back several cups of the broth as was, almost clear with just a touch of parsley and some seasoning. It's delicious but the best thing is: You know have a highly flavoursome stock, perfect for freezing and even more perfect for risotto. The remainder of the cooked chicken is also great for the risotto, but that's yet another story (see page 88).

---

tikka your breath away
chicken kebab

BORNE of laziness rather than necessity, my moreish chicken tikka kebab came about one Saturday evening when I discovered a couple of chicken breasts still marinating in the fridge from the night before. Loath to waste the meat (I had initially planned on scoffing them in a chicken tikka masala (*see page 131*) on the Friday but had filled up on Irish tapas – crisps and nuts), the next day I decided to cook them off, but not go the whole masala curry monty. Instead of making a saucy meal out of it, I cooked the pieces on a griddle pan and filled some pitta pockets. The resulting kebab was so delicious it immediately became a favourite. Sweet and tangy, this is a great light lunch or supper.

Punjabi in origin, chicken tikka is traditionally baked on metal skewers in a hot clay based oven called a tandoor after a time marinating in yoghurt and spices. The literal meaning of tikka in Persian – the language of the Mughals who named many Indian dishes – is "pieces."

The pieces are also traditionally brushed with ghee (clarified butter) at intervals, but in my world, this constitutes a bit of a mission so the griddle pan is as complicated as I go.

INGREDIENTS (for the tikka)

3 chicken breasts, chopped into large, same-sized chunks
400ml tub of natural yoghurt
2 tbsp of garam masala
tbsp of tomato purée

1 tsp of paprika
1 tsp of sugar
1 tsp of ground cumin
1 tsp of ground coriander
1 tsp of chill powder
1 tsp of mustard seeds
3 cloves of garlic
thumb sized piece of ginger
good splash of sunflower oil
2 red chillies, finely chopped

FOR THE SANDWICH

chopped coriander
pitta pockets or nan breads
chopped spring onions
chopped tomatoes
shredded iceberg lettuce
mayo or riata

THE PLAN

First of all, grate your garlic and ginger and place in a bowl. Finely chopped the chilli (taking care not to wipe your eye or pick your nose) and mix into the garlic/ginger.

Add the splash of oil to a frying pan and add the mustard seeds. When they start popping, remove from the heat and pour the seeds and oil into the garlic/ginger/chilli mix along with the paprika, cumin, coriander, chilli powder, tomato purée, sugar and garam masala. Give a good mix and allow to cool. Add your yoghurt and combine and then add the chicken pieces. Make sure all the chicken is coated in the tikka mixture and then cover with clingfilm and bang in the fridge, ideally over night.

After the marinating period, all you have to do is cook off the chicken and assemble the sandwich – the latter I won't insult your intelligence by explaining.

To cook the chicken you can either roast it in a hot oven, cook under the grill or blast on a griddle pan – which I do, because it's quick and handy. It's a good idea to skewer up the chicken first because then it's easier to turn, but again I just give it some attention on the griddle and it's fine. About six or seven minutes turning on a high heat and it should be done.

It should also smell divine as it sears and so long as you don't over-fire the chicken, a big nan or pitta filled with succulent, meaty chunks and some crunchy salad should tikka your breath away.

nine... sundays

the diet might have to wait
melting lamb shanks

I HAVE come to the decision that turkey is a vastly over-rated food source. Tradition is being sacrificed for taste and I reckon, if it wasn't for Christmas, we'd hardly eat it even once a year.

As much care as you take with the buying, preparation and eventual cooking, even the best turkey isn't going to be as succulent as a decent chicken. It's just too darn dry. The best of the best turkey is just, well, less dry.

I had my epiphany earlier one year when I took a notion for lamb shanks. I picked up four meaty little chunks for a pound a pop at a local butchers, enough to feed four people (with varied accoutrements of course). After digging out a recipe, I braised them slowly in the oven for two hours until the meat was literally, falling off the bone. I didn't give it much of a chance to fall though, scoffing the tender flesh with some mashed spuds and a gravy reduction before you could say, "Pass the cranberry, this turkey's a bit on the dry side."

At a fraction of the cost of a medium-sized free range turkey, with a fraction of the preparation and taking fraction of the cooking time, the lamb shanks were taste-eons away from the meat of a dry festive bird. They were so delicious in fact, I have decided to have them regularly – as regular, as regular could be.

INGREDIENTS

4-8 lamb shanks (this recipe will have loads of leftover gravy if you only cook 4 shanks but is ample lubricant for 8)
500ml of chicken stock
300 ml of white or red wine (I've tried it with both and they're equally great)
2 tbsp of plain flour
1 tbsp of sun-dried tomato paste
dash of olive oil
big sprig of rosemary
2 bay leaves
pinch of thyme
1 large onion, roughly chopped
1 large carrot, roughly chopped
2 cloves of garlic, chopped

THE PLAN

Start off by frying up the lamb in the oil in a large frying pan or flame-proof casserole dish. Don't be afraid to give it a good blast as it is this caramelisation

which will give the resulting gravy its potency.

After about 10 minutes, remove from the pan and add the onions and carrots. Give these a little colour and your cooking is almost done.

Dump the meat, carrots and onions into a casserole dish. Stir in the flour, garlic, sun-dried tomato paste, thyme, rosemary, bay leaves, stock and wine. Add a pinch of salt and pepper, stick a tight-fitting lid on and bag it into the oven for one and half hours at 160°C.

After that time, check the shanks. If they're falling apart they're done. If not give them another half hour.

Then, remove these from the casserole, strain the gravy into another small pot and boil this rapidly for 10 minutes or so until the sauce is thick and glossy. Add a knob of butter, check the seasoning and that's done too.

Serve the shanks on a castle of mashed potatoes with a moat of gravy and devour a length. You will want to take your time with this; the meat will be so tender it should melt in your mouth and if you aren't sucking the marrow out of the bones at the end, well, you're probably chewing through them.

You will want to take your time with this; the meat will be so tender it should melt in your mouth and if you aren't sucking the marrow out of the bones at the end, well, you're probably chewing through them.

american bickies
cookies, chocolate chip

COOKIE Monster was always a favourite character of mine from Sesame Street – and come to think of it that fella who lived in the bin, I can't remember his name. Actually, the Count wasn't bad either – a bit repetitive right enough – and Bert and Ernie had their moments.

The reason I mentioned the 'Monster' is because I ever since I first made the home-made versions, I can't seem to get enough of them. Very moreish and utterly decadent, these are a world away from the bland discs that comes in packets and are amazing with a cup of tea or coffee. Amazing.

When I first made these (I was following a recipe I cut out of one of the Sunday papers), I reckoned I would enjoy them more if I didn't know what was in them.

They contain a shocking amount of sugar and chocolate and butter. However this thought last as long as it took the first batch to bake, filling the house with a wonderful aroma as they slowly melted in the oven.

Considering they were the first attempt, I was chirpily pleased and the first bite reaffirmed my suspicions. Yes, I am the Cookie Monster reborn.

This recipe makes loads of cookies, though the cookie dough (also delicious by the way), lived happily in the fridge for three days. I made a batch of eight each night, giving some away and duly polishing off the rest. They keep well in an airtight container to boot, so you can revisit your craving on a regular basis.

INGREDIENTS

220g of butter
210g of caster sugar
110g of brown sugar
1 tsp of vanilla extract
2 eggs
315g of plain flour
1 tsp salt
1 tsp baking powder
300g of your desired chocolate chips (I used white chocolate and milk)
150g of your chosen chopped nuts (I used walnuts)

THE PLAN

In a big bowl, start off by creaming the sugars, the vanilla and the butter – which will be infinitely easier if you allow the butter to come to room temperature. Add one egg at a time and mix like crazy until completely combined and fluffy.

In another bowl sift the flour, salt and baking powder and then fold gently into your eggy, sugary, buttery combo.

Lastly, add the chocolate and nuts and give it another quick mix. Cover with clingfilm and leave to chill out in the fridge.

Now, this is fun bit. Pre-heat the oven to 160°C and start to make your balls. In your hands, roll a desert spoonful of the cookie dough in a ball slightly smaller than a golf ball and place these on a greased baking tray some five or six centimetres apart. Bang this into the oven and wait for 12-15 minutes. The balls will melt and collapse leaving you with a flat cookie (and a wonderful smell in the kitchen).

After their allotted time, allow to cool slightly on a cooking rack before you dive in (in a culinary sense).

The perfect cookie, I have since discovered after cooking so many batches, is crispy around the outside and slightly chewing and moist in the centre.

COOKIES!

The following are some facts about Cookie Monster of which you might not be aware.

i). Cookie Monster's favourite cookies are chocolate chip.

ii). In a guest appearance on TV (apart from Sesame Street or The Muppets), Cookie Monster referred to himself as, "the Robert Downey Jr of cookies."

iii). Before he turned into the Cookie Monster, his name used to be Sid.

---

nothing compares to you
potato bread

NOTHING compares to home-made potato farls. Even the best of the best in packet form are nowhere near as succulent and as satisfying as those you can knock up at home for a fraction of the price.

Tatty scones, as my mother calls them, are best eaten straight from the pan, hosed in melted butter with a sprinkling of sea-salt, blindingly hot and homely. Of course, if you're making more than a few, it's a good idea to store the produce tucked into a folded tea-towel, for warmth – and you can always sample as you see fit.

You don't have to mess about with them either; no herbs, spices or embellishment. For the perfect potato farl, all you need are: spuds (obviously), butter, plain flour and seasoning – that's it – no cream, milk or fancy oils.

On the easiometer, potato bread can have the needle in the red, but only if you aren't vigilant. The secret is to keep and eye out and don't leave the pan, especially if you're trying to make thick ones, as I always am. The thicker, in my humble but gluttonous opinion, the better. Whether you're eating as is, with butter and seasoning or as part of a fry, thick potato bread has to be experienced to be believed. Slightly crispy outside and meltingly spuddy within, I would imagine even the Big Man upstairs is a fan.

Quantities for potato bread are hard to define, since I'm invariably making them with leftover mash. However, I always reckon the more potatoey they are the better, so one good ratio to bear in mind is one part flour to five parts mash. Again, the method here is what counts and once you've made your first batch, you'll soon get the hang of it and can adjust flour to suit. They're not fool proof (I've messed them up in the past) but if you take care, the hardest part will be resisting the little farls as they come off the pan. A side-less cast iron skillet would be the best thing to use, but I use a small, non-stick frying pan and I can't complain. Also, turning the little farls can be a bit difficult, so a fish slice or a palate knife will come in handy.

INGREDIENTS

whatever leftover mash you have. For argument sake, lefts say you've about 500g or roughly a pound
large knob of butter
tiny knob of butter
100g of plain flour, plus extra for dusting and rolling
salt and pepper

THE PLAN

If your left-over mash is cold, which, since it's leftover it's likely to be, melt the large knob of butter in the microwave and stir through the spuds with a generous sprinkling of seasoning and the 100g of plain flour. Give it a good mix up.

Next is the fun bit. Take a small handful of spud mixture and using a floured rolling pin and on a floured surface, roll out the farl to the thickness you want. I try to leave mine half an inch thick. Then on a medium heat, melt the tiny knob of butter and rub it around the pan with a piece of kitchen roll. You just want to coat the surface and no more.

Add the farl(s) and cook vigilantly for about 3 minutes per side. I always check after a minute in case the scone is colouring too much but basically you want to cook them until the flour has been cooked off. The thicker the farl, the lower the heat and the longer they'll take to cook through. It should take at least five minutes and again, possibly longer depending on thickness.

A good idea is to cook one and note how long it takes to colour and cook and then taste it to check for tastiness and the absence of flouryness. If they're too floury, give the next one an extra minute or so on either side and taste again.

The perfect tatty scone should be golden brown on both sides and piping hot inside but you'll know when you get it right.

Topped with a soft-pouched egg and a few brittle shards of streaky bacon and the meal goes beyond right.

GREEN GRAPE
1.49 Pound

BLACK
1.8

FRUIT

XX LARGE
ORANGE'S
4 FOR 1.00

LARGE
LEMON'S
3 FOR 1.00

WARNING
danger of suffocation.
Keep this bag away from babies
and children.

Sunderland

X

capital idea, old bean
mince and onion pie

STAGGERING through Sainsburys many moons ago I happened across the pie section. As usual, I didn't know what I was looking for until I found it but just then, an overwhelming notion came over me for a pie.

As soon as this thought was processed another popped it's head up: Pie Face. Remember him out of the Beano? I hadn't thought of Pie Face in years, with his pie bed spread, pie wallpaper covered in posters of pies and pie-shaped bedroom slippers. Of course, this reference will only apply to ladies and gents of a certain vintage but I loved Pie Face. He was a friend of Dennis's, if I remember correctly. But the thing that sticks in my head about Pie Face was that he used to have dreams that it was raining pies.

Anyway, I digress... Not knowing what you're looking for in a supermarket (until you find it) is an unnerving and sapping experience so when I found myself face-to-face with a whole section of meaty goodness in pie format, it felt as though I'd stumbled across a buried treasure.

Steak and Kidney, Chicken and Mushroom, Stout and Blue Cheese, Cornish Pasties, Mince and Onion, Scouse Pie, – I couldn't believe the selection. The next difficulty was deciding which one to buy but after consulting the back of the packs, I nearly fainted when I realised how high in calories and saturated goodness pies are. Steak and Kidney, I think, was the biggest offender at over 700 calories.

"Buy one immediately, Michael," my fat inner-child version of Pie Face piped up. "No, buy two, one for you and one for the missus and you know yourself, she won't fancy a pie and you'll have to eat them both."

Capital idea, old bean! And that was just what I did.

Unfortunately, after returning home, the heated, calorific bonanza of a pie didn't really live up to my expectations. I can't remember which brand the pie was – since I'd deliberated for so long – but suffice to say, I wasn't pleased with my choice of mince and onion. I resolved there and then to bake a pie of my own.

INGREDIENTS for Inner Pie Face's Mince and Onion

*This much filling fills a little tin pie dish I have, though the quantities can be adapted for larger or smaller dishes. If you make too much you can always freeze the remainder
glug of olive oil
400g of steak mince
2 onions, sliced
1 clove of garlic, crushed
pinch of dried chilli flakes
bay leaf
big pinch of fresh rosemary, finely chopped
tbsp of sun-dried tomato paste

about half a glass of red wine
half a pint of beef stock (if you're using a stock cube just use half the cube)
defrosted, ready-made, pre-rolled puff pasty (is there any other kind?)
egg, beaten

THE PLAN

Start off by frying up your onions in the olive oil on a medium to high heat. Don't be afraid to give them a bit of colour. That done (five mins or so), remove from the pan with a slotted spoon and turn up the heat. Next cook off the mince on a high heat until nicely browned. Return the onions to the pan, along with the garlic, chilli, bay leaf, sun-dried tomato paste, rosemary, red wine and stock. Simmer, partly covered for at least an hour, stirring every now and again. If it looks a little dry at any stage, just add a jag of water out of the kettle. But at the end, you want to have a very thick, porridge-like consistency. If needs be, a teaspoonful of Bisto and some cold water will thicken the mix. Allow to cool.

Then all you have to do is line your tin or pie dish with the puff pastry, fill to the brim with the mince and onion mix, egg-wash on the lid, pierce a hold in the top and bake in a hot over (225°C or there abouts, check the puff pastry packet) for 20 to 30 minutes or until the top is golden brown and irresistible.

With a big dollop of steaming mash, this is wondrous stuff, better than anything – and I mean anything – you can buy in the shops. Rich, satisfying and ultimately very tasty, a big wedge of this and you'll begin to understand where Pie Face was coming from.

convenience food
potato wedges

WE have an amiable and convenient arrangement in my house, one that is based on convention rather than hard and fast laws. The understanding is: I do the cooking and my other half does everything else.

Now, this might seem like an easy time of it for yours truly but there are bolt-ons to the cooking of course, like leaving out the wheelie bin of a wet evening or visiting the attic for whatever reason. Or, if I spill bolognese all over the kitchen floor, I'm expected to clear that up too (a job like this will be finished off to a higher specification when herself discovers what happened).

Similarly, Theresa is no stranger to the kettle and has been known to whip up a mighty fine salad during the summer months. Her signature dish is beans on toast with grated cheese and she also often lends a hand in an advisory capacity when we're deliberating on the merits of a future menu (ie, what we're having for supper).

But mostly, we stick to our jobs.

Weekday evenings are traditionally the hardest time for me and my domestication vocation. After my zombie like body has dragged itself across the threshold, supper must be organised and prepared. Again, this might not sound like much of a mission but my biggest undoing is not knowing what I want to eat until the time comes. We have no such thing as pork chop night or pasta night. The antidote to this, I find, is to have plenty of store cupboard ingredients on hand and then it only necessitates a brief stop at the shop to procure one or two The worst case scenario occurs when you arrive home from work only to realise that you're minus what you assumed was in the fridge.   Or, even more infuriatingly, if that certain item has turned the use by corner.

This next recipe was created on a whim once when I realised the only food we had in the house was spuds, cheese, ham and two kinds of onions, spring and normal. A trip to the shop was out of the question so it was kind of like Ready, Steady Cook only without the laughs or organisation.

Fortunately however, the resulting meal of herby potato wedges with ham and melted cheese was deeply, deeply satisfying and all the more gratifying because it was completely unexpected.

INGREDIENTS (for two)

4 big Cyprus spuds (these were the only ones I had and they worked a treat)
3 tbs. of olive oil
big pinch of mixed herbs
pinch of garlic salt
1 red onion, sliced
4 spring onions, chopped
2 handfuls of grated, mature cheddar cheese
pepper
2 small handfuls of chopped ham (bacon would also work)

heaped tbs. of light Philadelphia
dash of milk

First of all, give your spuds a good scrubbing. The wedges will hold together better if you don't peel them. Then chop them into wedges, along the longest part of the spud.

Drop the wedges into a large pan of salted, boiling water and simmer for 5 minutes. This will mean they won't take as long in the oven to cook through, but conceiveably, you could go straight to oven and forgo the boiling. I've done it many's a time.

Drain and then add two of the tablespoons of olive oil, the garlic salt, the mixed herbs and a good grind of black pepper.

Mix gently trying not to break the spuds up too much, spread evenly over a baking sheet and bake in a pre-heated oven (at 190°C) for 10 minutes.

Whilst this is happening, fry your sliced onion in the other dash of olive oil until golden.

After the spuds have been going for 10 minutes, remove from the oven and turn each of them over. Return to the oven for another five minutes or until tender.

Whilst this is happening, combine the Philadelphia and the milk and mix thoroughly.

Divide the wedges between two bowls, sprinkle over the ham, the fried onions, spring onions and the cheese then put the bowls in the (probably) still very hot oven – you don't have to keep it going – to allow the cheese to melt slightly.

Now, you might have been wondering about the milk and Philly combo. After the cheese has started to melt, remove the bowls from the oven and drizzle over the runny cheese mix. Add another touch of seasoning and that's it.

I was going to say this is the quickest and easiest supper you'll cook all year, but I won't: I don't want to give herself the wrong idea!

winter warmer
hungarian stew

A FRIEND brought me a Hungarian sausage back from his holidays some years ago; the only thing was, he'd gone nowhere near Hungary. He'd gone to Cork.

Nevertheless, we (that is, my stomach and I) were more than appreciative of the gesture, and after some subsequent investigations we discovered that it actually had originated in Hungary, arriving in Cork by way of a friend of a friend (or something along those lines).

Similar to the Spanish chorizo in looks and taste, the sausage, which I suspect was a 'csaba' if the photos on the internet are anything to go by, was delightfully toothsome stuff (thanks again Olly). I started off by chopping off a few slices and scoffing them cold and unadulterated by the kitchen window. A lot softer than chorizo and containing substantially fewer chunks of fat, the sausage almost disappeared there and then. Slightly sweet and deeply smoky, I had visions of adding it to pizza or even roasting the whole thing in the oven. In the end, to use it up and also to prevent me from devouring the entire sausage there and then, I decided I'd make a stew and freeze some of it. This resulting recipe is for Impromptu Hungarian Stew. Comforting and satisfying in equal measure, it's the kind of stuff I can imagine eating for supper in early autumn when the chills have sneaked back into the air and we're expecting that first frost.

INGREDIENTS (for four)

1 Hungarian sausage, thickly sliced (or, if you don't have a friend called Olly who knows a man in Cork, who knows a man, a chorizo will do nicely – in which case it becomes Impromptu Spanish Stew)
1 can of chopped tomatoes
sprig of thyme
bay leaf
teaspoon of hot smoked paprika
chopped parsley
2 cloves of garlic, chopped
1 onion, chopped
4 rashers of streaky bacon, chopped
half a glass of red wine
1 can of any of the following, chickpeas, cannellini beans, butter beans
pint of chicken stock
1 dried chilli, crushed or chopped
a couple of handfuls of diced waxy potatoes (about 10 to 15 oz) – the waxies will keep the shape better
good glug of olive oil

First of all, start the bacon in the olive oil in a large, heavy-based pan until it starts to crisp up, then add the sausage.

Turn the heat down to medium and allow the sausage to lose some of it's juice, give it about two minutes. Now add the onion and garlic, turn it down low and allow to sweat until soft, about five minutes.

Fling in the can of tomatoes, the paprika, wine, bay leaf, sprig of thyme (don't worry about chopping or de-leafing the stewing will do that for you and then you just have to retrieve the twig), the chilli, the potatoes and the chicken stock. Give it a good grind of pepper, stir it up, bring to the boil and simmer for about 30 minutes or until the sauce has thickened slightly and the potatoes are cooked through. Now add in the can of pulses (chickpeas or whatever) give it another two or three minutes, and then taste for seasoning – remember bacon will be salty.

It should smell wonderful from moment one but at this stage, such will be the aromas filling your kitchen, you'll be gagging to get stuck in. Take a deep breath and calm yersel. Then just before you're about to serve, toss in a handful of chopped parsley and stir it up.

Crusty break will work a treat at soaking up the unctuous juices as would rice or even mashed potatoes.

Divide among four bowls and devour immediately without speaking.

Needless to say, I didn't get freezing a drop.

IT'S funny the way the world works sometimes; just think of Sunday dinners. You go to all the trouble of preparing a roast chicken, boiling spuds, fixing the stuffing, roasting carrots and making gravy. And then, when all is said, done and scoffed, which part do you enjoy the most? For me at least it's almost always the stuffing and gravy combination (apart from the chicken skin which is beyond ambrosial).

As good as the chicken or mash or veggies can be, they're often only a receptacle or a carrier of the taste – the real relish being the succulent stuffing and rich gravy. No wonder I used to love the silver tray of chip, pea, stuffing and gravy after a good night out – although granted, this combo used to taste a lot better after you'd numbed up your taste buds with a few cold beverages.

The same applies, again for me at least, with the roast beef and Yorkshire puddings of this world. As delicious as the meat can be, I regularly find myself yearning for just one more Yorkie (the pudding, not the bar) to soak up the gravy. Crispy on top, where the cap often seems to rise and fall away to the side like a weird toadstool and soft and bread-like at its base – sodden with taste-bearing gravy – the perfect Yorkshire pudding is just about the highlight of any roast dinner.

I have therefore discovered, that it is always prudent to make twice as many puddings as you think you'll need. For example, if you're cooking for eight people, you're going to need at least 16 Yorkies.

Worlds away from the frozen crap you'll buy in the shops, self-generated Yorkshire puddings are the only way to go – unless you've a butler who'll make them for you. The following recipe should make four big Yorkies but you can double or treble the ingredients as necessary.

INGREDIENTS

two large eggs and a separate egg yolk
100g of plain flour
250ml of full fat milk
sunflower oil or beef dripping
pinch of salt

THE PLAN

The absolute key here is to get the oil, whether you're using the sunflower or beef dripping, as hot as possible. You will also get better results if you use a metal tray for your Yorkies. I use a muffin tin and up until now (fingers crossed whilst touching wood) they never fail to rise.

So before you do anything else, pour one centimetre of your choice of oil into each of your muffin tin spaces and bang the tray into a preheated oven. The oil needs to heat for at least 10 minutes until it's very, very hot.

Now make your batter. Ideally, you'd want to have this prepared the night before, but in my disorganised world, this is very rarely possible. So if you forget, don't worry, they should still be class.

In a large mixing bowl, dump in the flour, make a well in the centre, add the eggs and slowly whisk in the milk. You want a kind of runny batter, sort of like paint. Add a large pinch of salt and it's done.

Then, when your oil is sufficiently hot, retrieve from the oven and pour the batter into each space, right on top of the oil. You'll know if the oil is hot enough because it should sizzle nicely. Work quickly at this stage, to keep the oil hot, and get the tray filled and back into the oven as soon as possible.

Cook for at least 20 minutes and the Yorkies should rise, crisp and golden up and become utterly irresistible.

VARIATIONS

For a change, try adding a dollop of wholegrain mustard to your batter at the mixing stage. Or, you can even have these bad boys for breakfast; with a sausage, another egg and a bit of bacon sticking out of the top, all you need is a squirt of tomato ketchup and your in taste heaven.

Or for the in ultimate weight gain – and taste – make a normal Yorkshire pudding and serve it as a hot dessert with a big spoonful of creme fraiche and a drizzle of maple syrup or runny honey.

Crispy on top, where the cap often seems to rise and fall away to the side like a weird toadstool and soft and bread-like at its base – sodden with taste-bearing gravy – the perfect Yorkshire pudding is just about the highlight of any roast dinner.

ten... going veggie, almost

crunchy, succulent and moreish
sweetcorn

I KNOW I might have suggested earlier – probably over-enthusiastically and certainly naively – that certain kitchen aromas are my favourites of all time. Hot chips with cheap malt vinegar springs to mind, or baking bread, torn open and steaming; onions frying or spluttering bacon or freshly ground coffee brewing – I'm already salivating at my nasal hallucinations. But, as Christopher Lambert was fond of saying, 'There can be only one'.

If I had to pick one smell, just one smell I could take with me to a desert island and treasure it forever, there would be very little consideration required.

I bought two big corn-on-the-cobs last week from a local supermarket and boiled them up for 10 minutes or so before liberally spreading them with real butter, adding a dusting of salt and pepper and I swear to God, I nearly passed out at the scent of them. I actually laughed out loud at the thought of the missus landing back to find me sprawled all over the kitchen floor, cobs and legs akimbo, butter all over the place and a big stupid grin on my face.

I must have sat at the kitchen table for a full minute, my nose millimetres from the yellowest of yellow kernels just inhaling the deeply tantalising aroma and saying "Ahhhhhhh," like some kind of half-cut eejit.

The rational side of me knows that this smell is essentially hot butter and the corn side of things only has a minimal part to play. But I don't care.

Sweetcorn holds no small amount of nostalgic significance for me too. My grandmother used to make them for myself and my brother on clear autumn evenings when she was trying to tempt us into the house for some heat. Every time I smell al dente corn on the cob, I am magically whisked back to a time when the world was infinitely simpler and pleasures arrived in the form of blisteringly hot corn and a melting '99 from the man in the van.

However, if there's one thing better than smelling hot cobs with butter, it's eating hot cobs with butter: Crunchy, succulent and moreish. I often think that tastes this special can't be good for me and of course they aren't, considering the chunks of butter I'm liberally applying – it has to be real butter too, not the hydrogenated vegetable stuff – it's not as if you're eating it morning, noon and all through the night. My grandmother also used to say that: "There's only enough butter on your bread if you can see your teeth marks on it." Similarly, there's only enough butter on your corn if there's a puddle on your plate.

Despite that introductory smelling period I invariably burn the roof of my mouth before the corn gets a chance to cool down. Every single time. It's the hot pizza syndrome. But I don't care about that either.

Later on in the evening when my mouth blisters and I'm still picking renegade slivers of kernal out of my incisors, I take solace in the memory of the corn and wonder when I can buy more. I'll also wonder for the umpteenth time if corn is dif-

ficult to grow and more importantly, if the missus will let me. I wonder...

INGREDIENTS

As many corn-on-the-cobs as you can lay your hands on
loads of butter
salt
pepper

THE PLAN

Indulge your senses.

hummus – broadly speaking
broad bean pate

HANNIBAL the Cannibal liked them and if they're good enough for Dr Lecter...

After spuds, asparagus, sweetcorn and onion (bhajis) broad beans are my favouritest vegetables. Perhaps, they have attained this venerated position because I only get them for a brief time each year – who knows – but whatever the reason, they're class. They're so deliciously distinctive and robust and you don't even have to mess around with them to enjoy the best of what they have to offer. Simply blanched and tossed in lemon juice, olive oil and a sprinkling of salt and pepper, and they make the most wonderful topping for bruschetta - perfect with a nice chianti, as the good doctor might say. I can even eat them straight out of the bowl.

Broad beans are in season from late spring onwards and that is the time if you don't want your beans to taste of haulage and airmiles.

The oldest of all our beans, the broads or the favas have been cherished since the stone age. Once upon a time, they were even important enough to warrant the death sentence if they were 'tea-leafed' from open fields.

Prevalent throughout the Med and the Middle East, they are traditionally eaten raw in Greece. Peeled and scoffed as is, the little kidney shaped greenies are often washed down with a swig of Ouzo.

As is the case with peas and asparagus, the sooner you eat broad beans after they're picked the better. The longer they languish in the fridge, the more of their succulent sugar turns to starch. Older beans also develop a tougher skin, but you can simply rid yourself of this prob by blanching and peeling. Granted, this is a bit of a mission but I find a glass of the aforementioned chianti helps.

The following recipe for broad bean pate is simplicity itself and makes for a great topping for bruschetta (*see recipe on page 42*) or rustic bread. This is the kind of food I have on a sunny Saturday afternoon when there's nothing on the telly. It's like hummus, broadly speaking.

INGREDIENTS

500g broad beans, shelled
1 or 2 cloves garlic, crushed
1 tsp ground coriander
1 tsp ground cumin
1 tsp turmeric
juice of half a lemon
2 good glugs of extra virgin olive oil, roughly 4tbsp
seasoning to taste

Dump the beans in boiling water and simmer until tender, about 5 minutes. Drain but reserve the stock.

Place the beans and spices in a blender and blitz until mixed, about 10 seconds should do it.

Add the lemon juice and garlic and using the stock, thin the mixture with a little to form a thick purée. Then gradually stir in the oil a little at a time and that's it.

I normally give this a little resting time in the fridge before seasoning. Dust with a little more turmeric and it's good to go (down your gullet). And depending on how thick or thin the pate is, you can even use it as a dip for breadsticks or toasted pittas or even crisps.

This pate is also best friends with beer, funnily enough.

---

getting your curry fix...
a great dahl

HEADING into final year at university, I moved to Portstewart with a few friends; it was make or break time. There could be no more messing around; no more heading down town for happy hour in a suit because there was nothing else clean; no more drinking beer in the afternoons because you'd slept in for your 2pm lecture; no more hide and seek around the house when the beer had run out. In short, there was to be no more messing around.

But more importantly, curry fanatics to a man, we were delighted to discover that a delivery service was available from the local curry house, the Ashiana Tandoori, situated on the Diamond in the centre of town. The world had never seen four students this excited, especially when the (student) loans came through. For four lads whose culinary prowess stretched to an egg-in-a-cup and toast (we used to buy flats of eggs with 24 in the pack), or chopping Pepperami onto gigantic pizzas, the Ashiana was a Godsend and perfectly affordable if we went Dutch, which we invariably did.

We promptly stuck up a copy of the Ashiana menu and crossed off each curry as we had it delivered. The chicken bhuna was my personal favourite, deep, earthy and ambrosial and it went perfectly with a handful of chips and half a garlic nan.

Dhansaks and jalfrezis were also popular, although we only tried the vindaloo that once – but that's another story.

Authentic to a fault, the Ashiana has since closed down but in its hey-day was a bustling, award winning eatery, sumptuous within and toothsome without. It was so good in fact, it had an indelible effect on my appetite and I have been rustling up curries at home ever since.

This next recipe, whilst not as authentic as the good ole days at the Ashiana, is definitely worthwhile as a winter warmer when you can't be bothered going the whole hog with spices, meat and all the rest.

Super quick and deeply satisfying, this lentil dhal can be made with whatever curry paste you like, though I've tried it with tikka masala and madras and they both work really well.

INGREDIENTS

200g of red lentils
good glug of sunflower oil
two cloves of garlic, crushed
one large onion, finely chopped
1 chilli pepper, also finely chopped
two heaped tablespoons of curry paste, tikka masala or madras or whatever
half a cinnamon stick
the juice of half a lemon (or lime)
100ml of coconut milk
100ml of double cream
one litre of water
can of tomatoes, drained
big pinch of sugar
coriander for sprinkling

THE PLAN

Wash the lentils and leave to drain. In a heavy bottomed sauce pan, sweat the onion and garlic and chilli pepper in the oil on a low heat until soft.

Next, turn the heat up a little and add the curry paste and the lentils. Stir fry for a minute or, stirring to coat everything nicely and then dump in the tomatoes with the big pinch of sugar, the cinnamon stick, the hot water and the juice of half the lemon or lime. Bring to a slow simmer, and bubble, stirring from time to time for 15 minutes or until the lentils are puffed up and cooked through.

You might need a little dash of extra water if it gets too dry but the consistency should be like that of a really thick soup.

Lastly, stir in the creams, give it another minute or so to reduce a little and that's it. Check the seasoning – it might need another touch of sugar – sprinkle on the chopped coriander and tuck in.

This goes unbelievably well with some pilau rice, popadoms, nan bread, mango chutney and a bottle of Kingfisher.

Sometimes, for old time sake, I eat the left overs for breakfast. And that would tighten ye!

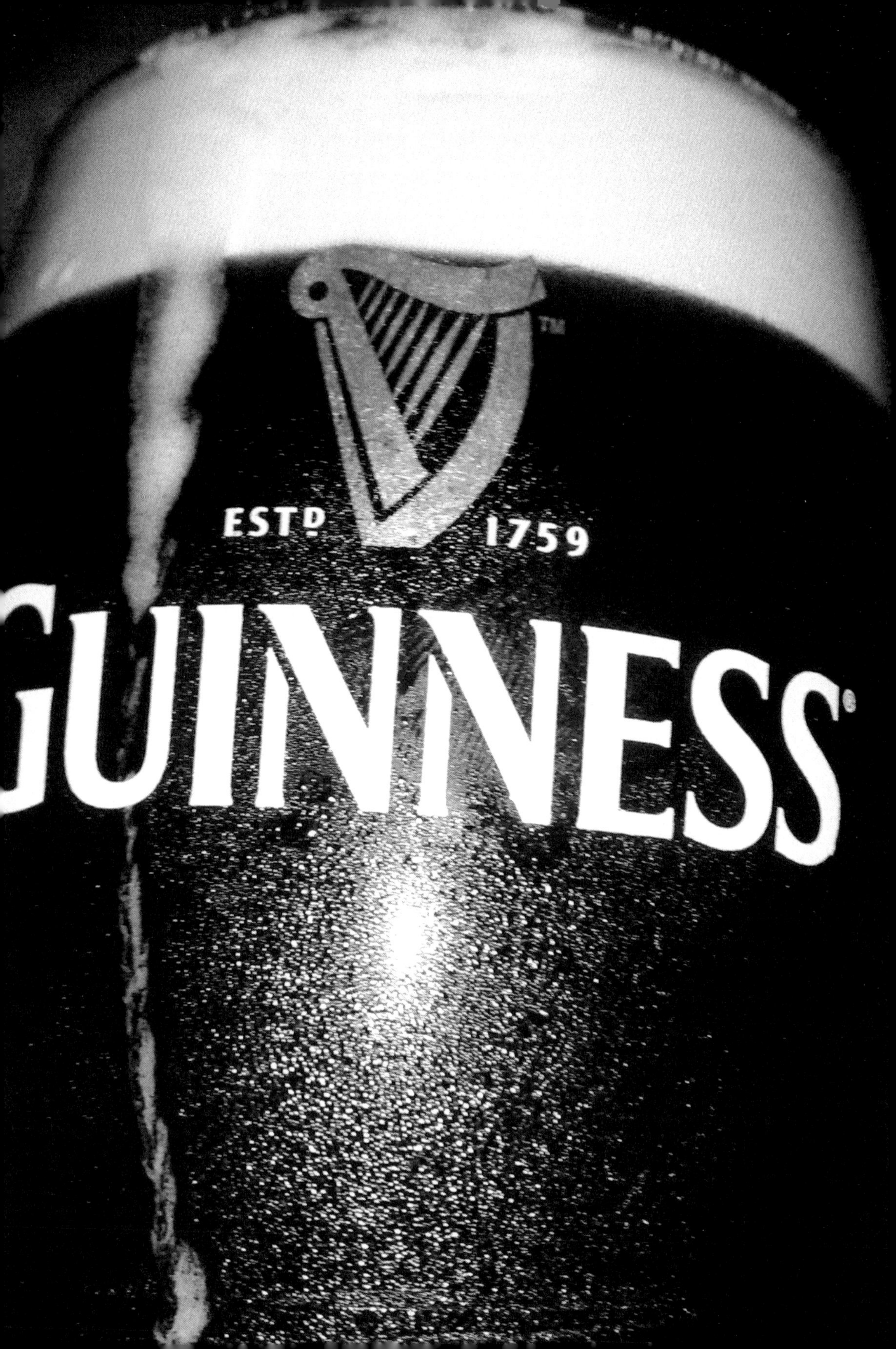
ESTD 1759
GUINNESS

roasted and red and delicious
spanish style peppers

SOMETIMES it's just too hot to cook. Not that we enjoy much of a summer to mention but there are usually a few days every year when my anti-perspirant was tested to the limit (ie, it didn't work and I looked like that lad off the Lynx ad).

Melting faster than femake hearts at a Rod Stewart concert, I habitually find myself adrift in the kitchen on a clammy Tuesday evening wondering what could be worth the effort. Spuds are out, as is pasta, risotto and just abut anything that requires standing over the hob. But faster than you can say, "Quick! Get the matches and charcoal!" The heavens usually open and we are once again confined to the house. At least the rains the air, I suppose – every cloud and all that.

The heat also effects my appetite, I think. Could you imagine sitting down to a roast dinner or a mixed grill with a sheen of sweat coating your brow? Sometimes all you want is some left-over potato salad and a flash-fired fillet steak. Sometimes it's just too hot to cook.

This next recipe is perfect for sticky evenings (or afternoons) when you're glued to the sofa with the weekend on your mind. Ten minutes prep, a blast in the oven (when you're slacking your thirst) and the moment it takes to transfer to a plate, you'd be forgiven for wondering when your next holiday will be.

Roast red peppers with garlic, tomatoes and anchovies is such an experience, once you've tried it, you might find yourself longing for clammy weather. This is also a cracker when you find yourself in need of a blast of sunshine in the dead of winter.

INGREDIENTS (for two a main or four as a starter)

4 big red bell peppers (they have to be red, the yellow and green ones don't work half as well)
1 birdseye chilli, finely sliced
4/6 tomatoes, depending on size
8 anchovy fillets
2 cloves of garlic, finely sliced
handful of basil leaves, torn
extra virgin olive oil
crusty bread
big fat glass of slightly chilled rioja (to serve)

THE PLAN

Split the peppers in half, down the line of the green stalk if there is one. Whilst the stalk isn't edible (trust me), keeping it on helps the pepper retain its shape in the oven. Scrape out the innards and seeds and lay the peppers hole side up in a lightly oiled casserole dish – the more snugly they fit the better.

Now, if you've ever done this recipe before, you may be tempted to boil the kettle and skin the tomatoes but in Michael's world, life is too short for skinning tomatoes. I just quarter them and add them to the mouths of the peppers.

Next, cut each anchovy fillet in three and add these to the peppers; just sit them on top of the tomatoes. Divide the garlic slices among the peppers, tucking some underneath the tomatoes and anchovies and do the same with half the amount of your torn basil (reserve some for sprinkling at the end of the cooking) and the birdseye chilli pieces.

Then, when all the pepper halves have their payloads of garlic, basil, anchovies, chilli and tomatoes, drizzle about a tablespoonful of your olive oil into each one and add a good grind of pepper – but no salt, the anchovies will take care of that.

Place the casserole dish in a pre-heated oven (210°C) for 10 minutes and then turn the heat down to 180°C and continue to cook for about 40 to 50 minutes. Check them after 40 minutes and if they're slightly charred along the edges and collapsed, they're ready.

Remove (carefully) from the casserole and transfer to plates, pouring all the remaining juices over the tops of the laden peppers.

Allow them to cool slightly and then sprinkle over with the rest of the torn basil and serve with the crusty bread and that big glass of wine.

Sunshine on a rainy day...

not to be confused with the mexican tortilla

I WAS introduced to tortilla a few years ago in Dublin, and I simply could not believe the taste; it was a revelation. It was at a party actually, and I made the sublime faux pas of commending the hostess on this new, exquisite foodstuff I had never experienced before. I made a real big deal about it, ranting and raving about the simple and yet hugely delicious flavour.

As it happened, it was the only thing she hadn't prepared – and to make matters worse, her Spanish sister-in-law had brought it along and (as I later realised), the two ladies disliked one another – immensely.

Despite eating it at every opportunity since (which wasn't often enough), it wasn't until quite recently that I decided to have a crack at one of my own sweet-onion-laced potato omelette cakes. For some reason, I imagined it would be all too time consuming and complicated and I suspected the recipe would be a highly guarded secret. It wasn't until I witnessed a slap-dash Hugh Fernley Whittingstall preparing one prior to a drinking session, that my damascene moment arrived and even then, I wasn't confident of the final taste until I was eating.

Also known as Spanish omelette, tortilla is not to be confused with the Mexican grub of the same name, but more about that another time. If ever something was worth the effort, this is it. And to add compliment to convalescence, since it's essentially only spuds, onions, olive oil and eggs, it's honest to goodness the best stuff you could be munching. I've tried adding little twists along the way like pancetta, ham, chorizo, peppers and spinach but the original is still very much the best. If it's not broke, don't break it.

INGREDIENTS

1 large onion
300g small waxy potatoes like Charlotte or Pink Fir Apples
4 tablespoons olive oil (or there abouts)
6 large eggs (preferably organic and free range)
salt and freshly milled black pepper
hot smoked paprika, half teaspoon
You'll want a frying pan with a lid for this recipe. A medium sized one, around 20 cm in diameter would be perfect. WARNING: If you use a bad pan, this will stick. Guaranteed.

THE PLAN

Thinly slice the onion and then peel the potatoes and do likewise. All the slicing done, dry the onions and spuds in a dry tea towel or some kitchen paper.

Heat three tablespoons of the olive oil in the frying pan until very hot and then add the potatoes and onions. Mix them around in the oil, then turn the heat down to the lowest setting, add a good grinding of salt and pepper, stick the lid on and cook gently for 25 minutes, or until the potatoes are cooked through. It's also a good idea to shake the pan from time to time, so that they don't brown too much. Ideally they want to almost poach in the pan as opposed to fry.

Next crack all the eggs into a bowl and combine with half a teaspoon of the smoked paprika. Season well and then add the cooked potatoes and onions (when they're cooked of course).

Return the frying pan to a medium heat and add the last tablespoon of oil. Mix the spuddy-onion-y eggy mixture well before dumping the whole shebang into the frying pan. Give it a shake to help things settle and then like before, turn the heat down to the lowest setting and let it sit without touching for at least 15 minutes or until the tortilla is set (ie there's no more liquid on the top).

and to add compliment to convalescence, since it's essentially only spuds, onions, olive oil and eggs, it's honest to goodness the best stuff you could be munching.

Let it rest for another few minutes and then turn it out onto a large plate. It should be cooked all the way through but ideally, it should still be slightly wet in the centre.

The more onions you've added the sweeter it will be and with a big glass of something red, tortilla is heaven itself. Even better the next day, this is arguably the best picnic food ever.

hai-ya!
chop salad

A STRANGE thing, the Irish salad; little mounds of ingredients spaced around a plate. Curls of ham, half a boiled egg, mounds of coleslaw, cheese or potato salad and maybe even a few whole cherry tomatoes – strange indeed – from the mound school of salads.

Most of us in this neck of the woods don't do very exciting salads but this is unsurprising really, when you consider that the Irish window of opportunity for eating cold things is only open for a few sunny days each year – if the window ever gets opened at all – what with the year round hail, sleet and snow. "Shut that wundy, were you born in a shed?" is a common phrase, even in July.

However, if you've ever visited the continent, you'll know how sumptuous and exciting salads can be – and not a mound in sight. This coming recipe is Corsican in origin, from a little restaurant in the mountains above Corté, U Spuntinu, which, I'm sorry to report doesn't exist anymore. The U Spuntinu Salad lived on the starters section of the menu but should really have been within the main courses, such was the substantial nature of the feast. I used to eat it as the precursor to a big bowl of pasta, but just a bowl of this stuff on its own is highly satisfying fare. You could even serve it up with steak, simply grilled chicken or even fish but I find some buttered wheaten bread works wonders as the crunch factor.

The quantities listed are enough for four people as a hearty supper but you'll be surprised how much you can get through. Crunchy, tasty and uber addictive. The gherkin, I find, adds a nice tang and the apple or pear makes a great natural sweetener. But, as always, you can leave out any ingredient you're not keen on and similarly, can add whatever you like as well, from beetroot to crispy bacon.

INGREDIENTS

1 gherkin
1 red pepper
3 spring onions
1 red chilli
1 medium red onion
10 cherry tomatoes
two hard-boiled eggs
1 apple or pear, peeled
1/2 a cucumber
large handful of crumbled feta cheese (or blue cheese if you're feeling saucy)
200g or there abouts of par-boiled baby potatoes
3 little gem lettuces
2 handfuls of fresh herbs (parsley, chives, mint or whatever you can get your hands on)
For the dressing

2 teaspoons Dijon mustard
3 tablespoons white wine vinegar or the juice of half a lemon
10 tablespoons extra virgin olive oil
Salt and freshly ground black pepper

THE PLAN

Give everything a good rinse under the tap and then let the chopping commence. It isn't rocket science, but just be prepared for a dishevelled kitchen. Obviously, you'll be discarding most of the seeds from the pepper and the chilli but it's kind of important to keep your chopping as uniformed as possible otherwise it'll look like a bit of a mess – albeit one you'll gladly clear up with your mouth.

Chop the onions and chilli as finely as you can but everything else can be done in 1cm pieces this goes for the lettuce as well.

When you're all chopped, combine everything in a big bowl and then mix up your dressing in a small glass, season to taste and then spoon some over your chopped salad. Taste and continue spooning until you think it's all dressed. You might not need all of it.

Serve immediately.

This is so healthy, you won't feel the slightest bit guilty for scoffing the lot.

IN early summer we invariably drift towards salads on warm Saturday afternoons. Crisp baby gems glistening with dressing and crunchy coleslaw with crumbly cheddar cheese – there's something so comforting about fresh, sweet leaves and raw vegetables. I think they might even be good for us.

As amazing as it may sound, not everyone likes salad. Off the top of my head I can think of at least three of my friends who wouldn't eat a slice of tomato or spring onion if their life depended on it. The stuff that breaks the trend of course, is potato salad.

Potato in salad format is one of those things that no two people will agree on. Should it be warm? Will it have floury or waxy spuds? Mayonnaise? Olive oil? Mustard? The list of combinations is long and argumentative and perhaps that is the great thing about spuds in general, the fact that they lend themselves to almost anything – except maybe custard or bananas.

So since potato salad falls squarely into the realm of personal taste, we can at least whittle it down to two main groupings - the waxy and the floury.

Once upon a time I was speaking to a friend about 'new spuds' as they are generally known and this friend of mine, voiced his preference for the floury variation. "Them wet ones," he told me with some venom, "I wouldn't even give them to the dog."

A bit strong, I think you might agree. But the thing that made it stick out in my mind was that I prefer waxy potatoes – that and the fact that his poor dog isn't getting dog-food.

Say what you like about waxy potatoes but for texture and taste, there are no substitutes. I have never been able to understand how people will fall over themselves for the floury kind. So they made good mash, but where's the taste? Charlotte or Pink Fir Apples are unbeatable in terms of taste – especially in salads.

Thus, when it comes to making potato salad (in my house at least), you will only ever find me using good waxy purdies. For a start, they don't turn into mash and also, they actually taste of something.

Again, the variations on potato salad are many and wondrous, so there is literally no end of recipes. The following recipe is one I picked up in Germany and goes particularly well with fillet steak. It's a bit of an effort, especially when you consider chips are the quintessential accompaniment with steak and they're as easy as boiling the kettle. Also, I've kept the amounts of ingredients purposely vague because it's the idea which counts really. Plus, you can never really have enough left-over potato salad.

The secret ingredient (well it isn't really a secret anymore) is the gherkin or small cornichons. I'd never have thought of adding these little pickled cucumbers to potatoes but once you've tried it, it's impossible to leave them out. The tangy vinegar adds a little bite which perfectly balances the creamy dressing. And if someone doesn't like gherkins – ignore them – chop them up really fine or even grate them and the offending picky person will never know they're there.

INGREDIENTS

A pot full of waxy potatoes
6 (or there abouts) rashers smoked, streaky bacon, grilled until crisp
1 large gherkin or several small cornichons
2 hard-boiled eggs, chopped
4 spring onions, chopped
salt and freshly ground black pepper
For the dressing
1 tbsp lemon juice
1 tbsp chopped chives
2 tbsp mayonnaise
2 tbsp soured cream or creme fraiche
1/2 tsp of french mustard

THE PLAN

Cook the potatoes in salted water until soft, then drain and return to the heat to dry out.

Then toss the potatoes with the crumbled crispy bacon, the diced cornichons, eggs and spring onions. Season well.

Fire together the remaining ingredients to make the dressing and mix enough of this into the salad to make it unctuous and delectable.

The main problem with this salad is refraining to eat the lot before it makes it the length of the table.

This is a meal on its own but with a rare steak and a glass of uber-cold weiss-bier, this is deadly stuff.

Once upon a time I was speaking to a friend about 'new spuds' as they are generally known and this friend of mine, voiced his preference for the floury varia-tion. "Them wet ones," he told me with some venom, "I wouldn't even give them to the dog."

food for the soul
apple crumble

AS desserts go, apple crumble has to be one of the finest. It's great because it's delicious and comforting but best of all, considering the amount of effort involved (not a lot) there's a huge amount of reward (happy days).

The trick, I think is to have the apple filling slightly too tart and the crispy crumble slightly too sweet and then somehow both variant textures and tastes meet in the middle in the most agreeable manner. Custard or cream or vanilla ice-cream helps too and you have to have it as soon as it's cooked, molten and lava-like, instant central heating to help cope with the worst Jack Frost can throw at us.

Bramley apples aren't much too look at but with a spoonful of sugar and some gentle bubbling, they are transformed into the most exquisite autumnal fare. The mixture too looks a little like baby food at first but that all changes when the crumble is added and cooked, golden, irresistible and bubbling around the edges.

You can basically crumble any seasonal fruit but good old fashioned apple crumble is hard to beat. I've tried it with raspberries and strawberries and I've tried pears and cinnamon; I've tried it with festive mincemeat but I'm always coming back to basics with a big bramley or two and some sugar. I've tried eating apples too but they just don't have the zing of a bramley. It is evidence, if ever we needed any, that simple things are often the best. Though in fairness, young braeburns make a good substitute.

INGREDIENTS (apple filling)

750g of bramley
40g of caster sugar
2 tbsp of water
INGREDIENTS (crispy crumble)
150g plain flour
75g butter, cubed
70g of light muscovado sugar
butter for greasing

THE PLAN

Working quickly – so they don't go too brown – peel and roughly chop the bramley apples and place in a saucepan with the water and sugar. Cook over a medium heat, stirring now and again for about seven or eight minutes or until the apples are tender and are starting to break down. Make sure to taste at this stage and if it's too tart add another sprinkling of sugar and taste again. Keep going until you get it how you like but keep it slightly tart. Dump your apple mix into your buttered pie dish, even out and set aside. (A one litre pie dish suits these quantities perfectly).

Pre-heat the oven to 180°C and next, make the crumble. Using your finger tips, rub the cubed butter into the flour until it looks like course breadcrumbs. The faster you can do this the crispier the crumble will be. Mix through the muscovado and it's ready. If you were of a mind you could always add a pinch or two of cinnamon but I like it plain and simple.

Spread the crumbled mix over the apple mix and place the dish in the oven. (You can prepare ahead to this stage and the crumble will live happily in the fridge for two days).

It should take roughly 30 minutes in the pre-heated oven until it's ready, golden and bubbling but the key here is to taste a little of the crumble to check that the flour has been cooked out. If it hasn't and it still tastes a little floury, give it another ten minutes.

I defy anyone not to be comforted.

bramley apples aren't much too look at but with a spoonful of sugar and some gentle bubbling, they are transformed into the most exquisite autumnal fare. The mixture too looks a little like baby food at first but that all changes when the crumble is added and cooked, golden, irresistible and bubbling around the edges.

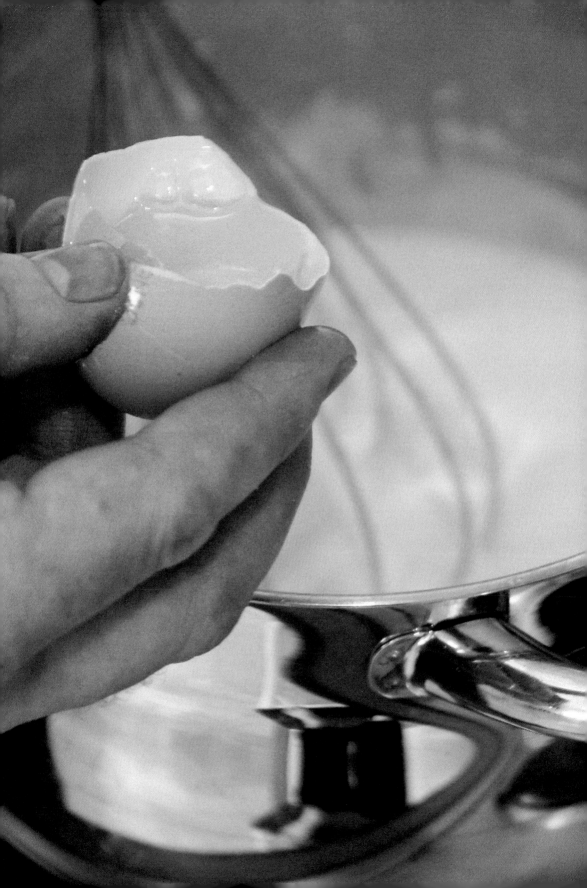

index... index... index... index...